Isaac Newton Lewis

Pleasant Hours in Sunny Lands in a Tour Around the World

Isaac Newton Lewis

Pleasant Hours in Sunny Lands in a Tour Around the World

ISBN/EAN: 9783337190668

Printed in Europe, USA, Canada, Australia, Japan

Cover: Foto ©Andreas Hilbeck / pixelio.de

More available books at **www.hansebooks.com**

Pleasant Hours in Sunny Lands

IN A

TOUR AROUND THE WORLD

BY

ISAAC NEWTON LEWIS, A.M., LL.B.

BOSTON
CUPPLES AND HURD
The Algonquin Press

1888,
By ISAAC NEWTON LEWIS.

TO LITTLE ANNIE MAY, WHOSE SILVERY LAUGH,
AND GENTLE, WINNING WAYS HAVE WARMED THE HEART
AND SOOTHED THE MIND, FOR MANY A VACANT HOUR,

These Pages are Gratefully Dedicated.

PLEASANT HOURS IN SUNNY LANDS.

CHAPTER I.

*Bright dreams of youth,
In living forms arise.*

MEMORY, like a perfume, permeates the sense and lovingly draws us to a grateful realization of its fond presence. Never so trivial the occasion, the influence is the same. Before me lies the unconscious agent of such renewed pleasure to-day. It is but an old newspaper, weather-beaten, yellow, and torn, but it speaks to me with more than earthly sweetness of past experience, thought to have been long since forgotten.

Rich labyrinths of palms and ferns, clouds of bright and delicately-tinted flowers, from earth to sky, spontaneously rise before my awakening mind in scenes too beautiful but for heaven, and even now fill the mind with wonder and the heart with joy. It is a Calcutta daily, bearing date of Sept. 5, 1887. On that day I had decided to leave northern India, and had taken passage for Madras on the French ss. Tibre, of the M. M. line. All that afternoon, under the guidance of an English pilot, we had slowly backed down the Hoogly, till we had reached Garden Reach, by the palaces and gardens of the King of Oudh, our mooring for the night.

One hundred wives has this old native king, all of whom, in return for his possessions up the river, are in royal style supported by the English government. The possibility of an enforced introduction to this motley and numerous household proved too much for my peace of mind, and had driven me to the cages of wild animals and the surrounding country for the few hours entertainment of enforced delay.

On the following morning, the early sun glanced through the heavy foliage with a power worthy of an Indian midsummer. Up and down, to and fro, floated the tall, light feather grass in the morning breeze, and made me long to be up and away.

Up and down the shaded deck, now watching the crowds of swarthy Hindoos openly bathing in the sacred stream, and now casting an admiring glance up at the beautiful French flag, gracefully floating in the air, we wore away the hours, until this, then bright and new, paper was handed me by the pilot, whose native servant had just arrived by rail from Calcutta with the latest news. It was a welcome guest, and fondly entertained by all those on board. How eagerly we all sought for news of home and friends! And now, to-day, from a mass of foreign correspondence, discolored, yellow and torn, it thrusts itself forward to the light, and mutely appeals for recognition. As then, I now read in the clear type of its title page:

"Passengers from Calcutta per ss. Tibre.

For Pondicherry, P. Farrin, Lt. Col. Godfrey and wife, Miss and Mrs. Dubern.

For Colombo, Mrs. Atkinson, Mr. Labousiere, wife and child, Le Pere de Wavre.

For Marseilles, Chauvin.

For Port Said, Isaac Newton Lewis.

For Madras, Kader Saib, Abdoul Gaffer."

These comprised the saloon. The many native passengers nearly all travelled either third class, or on deck, and probably thus saved their gold and silver with which to bedeck their bodies. The sight of that torn and faded souvenir of the East inspires me to jot down in some sort of way my many and varied experiences of that time, though I am fully aware that, as in moral experiences, the beauty and interest often lie too deep for expression. All personal narrative is, at the best, but the reflection of experience. To fairly represent the panorama which is constantly passing before the gaze of one in his world-wide travels is beyond human power, yet to friends and relatives, and to those who have neither the time, means, nor health to travel, something now and then may appear in these pages of interest, if not of profit. Like the clouds of eager doves swarming down on St. Mark's square in Venice, thoughts may crowd my mind but pass unnoticed. To me the experience is of more than earthly pleasure. To me it was worth my life to view the grandeur, sweetness, and profuse display of man and nature in the earth's broad circumference.

To see nature in all her wealth and loveliness, I knew, necessitated my meeting her at her home. With native man it is not a whit different, not with beast or bird. To accomplish this there is needed something more than money, something more than time. Health, intelligent attention and, not least, great physical and moral strength and courage. If you possess these, and a good command of the English, Spanish, German, French and Italian languages, you are well equipped for a world-wide tour, but not without. My college education came to my rescue on every emergency, and with the exception of the Hindustanee of India, I lost none of my precious time in study during my whole trip. Much wisdom is required in selecting your wardrobe, as well as pecuniary means. Warm wraps are as necessary, as light and firm clothing, for the tropics. In six hours and even less, the atmosphere may change from sultry to cool, from hot to wintry blast, but one valise for each hand is all in quantity that it is wise to carry. Much valuable time is often thus saved on trains and steamers, and ease of transportation as well as of stowing away in cabin, so greatly conducive to one's comfort and convenience, demands this. Three things are often forgotten in the outfit which are necessary to any enjoyable sea voyage, a good easy shoe or slipper for the feet, a powerful field-glass for the eye, and, most of all, a closely fitting hat or cap for the head. To suffer from the sun or to suffer from tight boots is equally unnecessary. If you are well equipped, though you pass through the Red Sea with the thermometer at 190 degrees, as it was August 9, 1887, or 160 degrees in the shade, as it was on my trip, you experience no actual suffering, but welcome everything with some degree of comfort. Heat and cold can be largely neutralized by proper diet, and by travelling first class on any respectable mail-boat, reasonable comfort and pleasure are always to be found.

CHAPTER II.

The sea, the deep blue sea.

No one realizes the maritime importance of such eastern ports as Boston and New York as the traveller. The tons of shipping, the majestic ocean steamers and the officious but necessary little tug boat soon disappear from view as one goes southward, and in but a feeble way appear again until you have travelled up the long Pacific coast to San Francisco. The same is nearly true in the Orient. Yokohama and Nagasaki in Japan, Shanghai and Hong Kong in China, Singapore and Penang in the tropical Straits Settlements, and Calcutta and Bombay in India, are the only ports on the Pacific and Indian oceans which furnish the traveller with anything like the busy scenes of even our contracted Boston. I took passage from New York one lovely morning in a long, trim steamship, lightly loaded—and as lightly officered and manned— the captain being a perfect gentleman, but with abilities that would have shone less dimly as a lecturer to a young men's literary club, who entrusted the navigation of the vessel to the third officer, aged about twenty years, whose common cry in a storm was " Come, gentlemen, please assist us to take in this sail," while his superior stood by dudishly twirling his eye glasses and smoothing an illfitting pair of yellow kids, intended to keep his hands from tanning. From Sandy Hook to Barnegat light the ocean looked its prettiest; but from that point to Cape Hatteras, where the Monitor went down during the war of the Rebellion, the boat played like a dolphin, pulling herself up here and rolling first on one side then on the other, till our heads pleaded for rest, and many a stomach for relief. My strong, good-natured Connecticut companion soon began to look worried, then anxious, and hastily retired below. The lovely, wide awake little widow, who had all the voyage entertained us with her wit and wisdom, suddenly ceased with a convulsive " I won't, there!" But she did. The sudden blanching of the face and a feeble look, half sickly, half frightened, led us to help her to seclusive preparation for so unequal a contest. The little girl and boy of one of the chief engineers, who had romped around the hurricane deck until they began to gasp and cry, were also beyond consolation. It was a complete triumph of the playful sea over boastful and self-willed man. Why I never suffered from sea sickness is beyond my comprehension. When I first perceive others falling under its influence, I throw myself completely under my strongest will power, and keep my imagination and senses under constant control. If that can account for my escape, it is well worth the fullest trial, for surely nothing can exceed the annoyance, the abject misery, both in feature, form and sense, than that of this bold enemy. Uniform, gay trappings, and kid gloves to our captain, pall upon the sight. The gallant third officer sighs for his mother and for but one square foot of her garden patch. But enough! Too much! Captain and third officer soon got on the bridge together, as a heavy fog loomed up and around us, making the passage extremely perilous, and the poor stricken passengers below trembled, as ever and anon they heard the shrill fog whistle shriek out the dismal warning of danger. The second day out, the sun was unbearable, the rays striking the flesh as if drawn by a powerful burning glass, so that all imprudent enough to forsake the awning were soon red and swollen on hands, neck and face, so as to be hardly recognizable. It was the severest lesson of the kind I have ever experienced, but it saved me from the scorching heat of India and Arabia farther on, and possibly from fatal injury from sun stroke. This day, and for days after, we were constantly welcomed by flying fish, dolphins and porpoises, but saw but very few vessels except schooners.

On the third day we met a brig bound for Europe, and a horrible man-eater in her wake. From the 23d parallel north latitude to the same parallel south, nothing is more common than this species of shark, and many a time I have seen a native swim out from the shore, with a long, sharp instrument between his teeth, until he had attracted the attention of this savage monster, and then cunningly snatching the weapon, with a lightning-like thrust, pierce his hated victim until the water grew red with blood. Alas for the unhappy native if he miss his first aim ; a furious lashing of the water, a heartrending shriek, and both fish and man quickly disappear from sight. Yet in Japan I afterward saw the shark commonly exposed in the markets for sale for food. A clear case of love for your enemies.

The fourth day out we sighted the Bermudas, lying low with an angry sea between. I was told that the Gulf Stream is 118 to 160 miles wide in this latitude, and that our crossing was nearly at right angles, to save time and coal.

When off St. Augustine, Florida, we met a West India steamer bound for New York, both of us rolling and pitching about in a way more alarming than amusing, while I could hardly see out of my eyes, they were so swollen from sun burn. Yet I could see with joy the fierce white caps, and the black, threatening thunder clouds lying low upon the horizon. Nothing at sea is so grand, so instinct with supernatural power, as a tropical hurricane. Bending low, as for a caress, the dark wind clouds gently kiss the slumbering sea till it glances up and smiles, when with one fierce swoop they clasp the deep in their strong embrace, and madly struggle to bear it heavenward.

Usually I arose before the sun, that no phenomena might escape me. I had reached the deck one bright morning, and on glancing toward the east, saw the sun just protruding above the horizon. The sea all around was glowing with warm color. Higher and higher rose the sun, gradually assuming the appearance of a golden balloon, until but a mere thread of gold held it to the sea Then, with a snap, upward darted the golden mass, leaving a pool of burnished gold in its bed beneath. Since then I have watched, but watched in vain, for the beautiful awakening to be repeated.

I have seen the heavenly bodies swing low at midnight in Arabia and Egypt, and shower upon my head their flow of dazzling meteors, until I stood transfixed at the magnificence of the display. I have seen, after days of fierce tempests, the mighty deep rise in its awful grandeur, until, darkly blue, it o'ertopped the masts and rolled upward in our track, so that it seemed that we must pierce its heaving mass or go to instant destruction, while roll after roll of seething foam fiercely pursued us from behind. Such I have seen, but in all my travels they have failed to appear a second time, and it so fills the mind with a sense of awe, of the feebleness of man, of the power of nature, that no single experience can suffice to satisfy intelligent man ; but perhaps it is better to have but once beheld than not at all, once to have felt the glow of heart and mind expanding towards the infinite and omnipotent.

The sixth day out, while looking over the rail, I discovered the largest and most beautiful nautilus I ever saw. Those found in the Pacific are mostly small and colorless, but this had large pink and blue sails, and was as large as a lady's hat. Its long tentacles reached down out of sight. It was under full sail and quite along side. Large sea turtles were sleeping on the surface of the water, and masses of seaweed and driftwood, such as Columbus met in 1492, indicated that we were close to San Salvador.

This in fact we reached in the afternoon. It was ominously still. No Indian to give us welcome. The Indian of Columbus is supplanted by the strong, lusty negro, who comes out with seashells, sponges, and a little fruit, and in passable English solicits your patronage. The sponge, when first brought up from the deep, is as black as ink, but on being boiled and dried, it assumes the common light and yellow color of commerce. There is nothing remarkable about the island in comparison with the many others of the Bahamas. All seem of coral formation, and at noonday each island glows like an emerald set in opal and sapphire. The green of the grass and foliage seems unnatural to a Northern man, and the rays of the sun turn the surrounding water, first into a yellowish border, then violet and greenish blue, down to the lively dark blue of deep water. To say that it is a heavenly scene is to describe it but faintly. The same beautiful panorama greeted me in the East Indies and afterwards in the Maldive islands in the Indian Ocean.

By night of that day, we made the new revolving light erected April, 1887, by the English on Watling's Island, a little southeast of San Salvador, and by some claimed as the first land discovered by Columbus in 1492. The following forenoon, Bird Island and lighthouse loomed up before us, followed by Fortune Island with its salt pans, bright shore and cosy verandas and cottages. Long before our arrival, on my glass, the keeper, his wife, and all his neighbors distinctly appeared around the base of the light, their dark figures and glistening eyes and teeth forming an amusing silhouette.

Tall cocoanut palms, with storm-bent forms, gracefully waved their plumed heads on high, while the cedar and mango trees tempted the sun-burnt traveller to seek their grateful shelter and rest. Conical huts of palm and thatch rose here and there, and, now and then, a blue or green villa with double veranda and varied awnings told of the presence of man. The glare of the noonday sun, and the opalescent hues of the shallow water, so combined the real with the canny that one had to pinch himself to be assured of wakefulness. As at previous points, we could find no harbor on account of the size of our vessel, but a row-boat, manned by six stalwart darkies, each like an ebony statue, soon was seen approaching for the mail we had brought from the States, followed by dugouts of fruit, coral and sponges, paddled by the same colored beings, dressed, when dressed at all, in bright colored ribbons and strips of cotton cloth.

After getting under way once more, we set our staysails to steady our now dangerously rolling vessel, and made for Cape Maysi, Cuba, passing Castle Island at eleven a. m of the same day, and leaving the mail, also leaving our own mail for the States. Here Capt. Kidd had his stronghold. Falling in with the trade winds, we made Baracoa and Cape Maysi the next day, where two steamers and several sailing vessels gladdened our eyes. We were then but 1237 miles from New York. Our experience in this land of misrule and Miss Don Juans was but a repetition of that in the Bahamas—plenty of hot sun, sweet fruits, beautiful colors and comely natives. There is some beautiful scenery in Cuba, but it is feeble compared with that of the opposite island of Hayti, which we visited the next day, and sailed from early morning to eve almost beneath the shadows of its lofty peaks and wooded slopes. Here at Port au Prince the natives, as well as the higher classes, make use of a sort of French language, while farther to the east of the same island the Spanish has equal adherents, so it is not an unusual experience to find a polyglot darky, whose importance and consciousness of the same somehow remind you of their uncultivated yet conspicuous wilds. These are the rendezvous of outlaw and slave, and seldom trod by foot of civilized man. Some of the ranges are, however, cultivated to their very summits, and had the heat not gone beyond 100 degrees, I would gladly have accepted an invitation to spend a month on shore, but my eyes were ever bent on the setting sun, so I bid adieu, and soon came to the only island owned by the United States or its citizens, in all this rich country. It is the island of Navassa, one of no great size, but of value. Its only commercial interest is its trade in guano. There were vessels loading under its high coast, but I passed it by with but a call, and gave myself up to the mild, delicious breezes of Jamaica.

Have you felt the inspiration of a coming shower after a sultry summer's day? Had you been with me, reclining at your ease and drinking in the spice-laden air that floated over the cooling water, permeating your clothing and stimulating your senses, however weary or ill in after-life, the memory would win a smile of peaceful satisfaction that you once had really lived.

But enough. Kingston is much like other places in the Indies, and needs no description. Its strong, finely formed men and bright, roguish children, all travelling to and fro with huge baskets or bundles on their brightly bedecked heads, are known to the world, so are its rare woods, its fruits and its fragrant spices; so we will on once more, with sails all set and breezes free, straight across the Caribbean Sea. Roll, roll!

splash, splash! and before night the hurricane, preceded by volley after volley of thunder, like a mighty hand down on your head, and simultaneous streaks and streams of lightning that fairly blind the eyes. One old sea captain comforted me with the story of one of his voyages here, when one of his men standing in my very position near the mainmast, was suddenly struck down without a mark or scar to indicate the cause. "But," said he, "you need not move, as these masts are of iron, which are never struck." Although my views coincided, I no longer felt interested in standing by a mast in a storm.

The Caribbean Sea is nothing in size compared with the Atlantic ocean, but it fills one with wonder that so much that is rascally and perilous can be forced upon one's defenceless head in such a little space. One clear, bright night, near Jamaica, in my study of the heavens, I came across that beautiful guide of the southern mariner, the Southern Cross. I have seen it often since, in its varied positions, but here, with the dipper and our polar star just disappearing in the north, its welcome gave unusual pleasure. From this time on constant surprises spring upon your attention in the gem-studded sky, until you are forced to regard them, in setting and form, as superior to the northern constellations. It is a wonderful inspiration that comes to one on a clear, still, tropical night, with starry gems floating their varied colors above, and sparkling animalculæ answering back from the disturbed sea below. Besides depth and brilliancy of color in both flora and fauna, the tropics also present greater grace and symmetry of form and deliciousness of perfume and flavor. It is the same at sea as on land. Even God's bow of promise holds the mind entranced. As it spontaneously broadens and brightens above the great sea, you in awe await the presence of the Most High. But such revelations are usually preceded by fierce gales and mighty upheavals of the deep, which prepare one as in no other way for the intense appreciation of the grand and beautiful.

It was after such a struggle of the elements, when parallel streams of electricity poured down before us, and the thunder rent our ears with pain, that we sighted the South American coast—a trackless wilderness. With marine glass in hand, I waited hours for some sign of civilization, when, on sweeping the horizon, my eyes fastened upon the waving cocoanut palms and trim cottages of Colon, the mouth of the Chagres river and Lessep's Panama Canal between. It lay so low its distance was soon overcome, and by sunset we were alongside of the wharf and mingling with the strangest crowd it has been my lot to meet. Ladies in silk and lace walked through the muddy streets, with nothing but a fan for head covering, side by side with the native Indians as quaintly robed as Eve in the garden of Eden, followed by the native garrison, composed, I should say, of a patriarch and his children and grandchildren, all dressed in the same sized uniform; so that while the scantiness of the older suggested coolness and rents, the generous length and fulness of the younger kept him in an inglorious perspiration, mostly under the heels of his immediate comrades.

Many of the scenes are far from humorous. Five deaths from the isthmus fever took place my first night; every little while two policemen shambled by, with a rough wooden box on their shoulders, with a companion bringing up the rear. A protruding arm or foot needed no explanation of the cause. No one is safe in the place. If it is not disease it may be evil human nature. Even the mosquito, that amusing little insect when in the North, becomes a perfect little fury here. You have not the heart to destroy, you know, even if your blows were as accurately as determinedly directed, so you gradually *pamper* the little creatures until, to put it mildly, you begin to look like a baby with canker rash and scarlet fever. If there is an exception, it is that the child has no contusions or facial protuberances arising from misguided views that the face, with a few active mosquitoes, can be pummeled at will with impunity. Despite the pests, we saw the town, the long dugouts at the market filled with fish, turtles, cocoanuts, plantains, bananas, mangos and yams, also the long, broad frogs croaking in the middle of the streets, and as large as the spanking hand of a modern school teacher, when seen through a misty veil of tears.

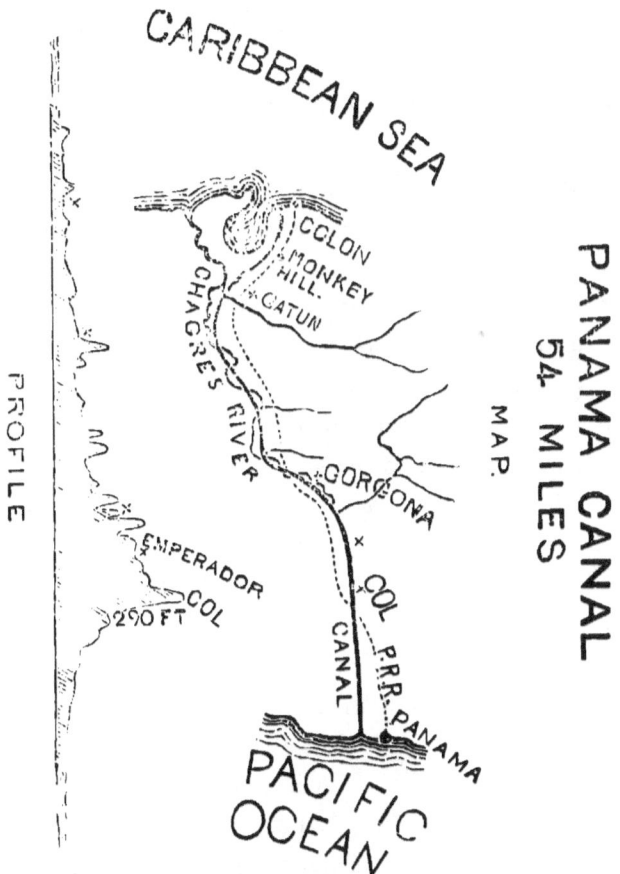

This place is also known as Aspinwall, after Capt. Aspinwall of New York, and is the northern terminus of both the Panama railroad and the canal, which the

French have for years been trying to construct to unite the Atlantic and Pacific. This canal was one of my chief objects of interest here, as I wished to compare it with the Suez, constructed by the same persevering and enterprising Lesseps. Only about thirteen miles are navigable, but the ground is broken nearly the whole distance to Panama, its southern terminus, and is easily distinguished by long lines of reddish soil peculiar to this section, contrasting with the light green of the herbage on the surface. No one here believes in the possibility of its completion. Machinery to the amount of thousands of dollars, unadapted to the work, lies exposed to the severe climate—a total loss. The whole country has been built up, and, at the two Obispos, pretty dwellings adorn the hill sides. If locks were to be introduced it would look some encouraging towards success, but to remove the mountains on the lower half to a level with the ocean will require more time and money than even the French national pride and energy will support. Lesseps had a comparatively easy task through the level sand plains of Eastern Egypt, where the Bitter Lakes and ancient canal from Cairo to Suez only needed widening and deepening, but here, rock, mountain, river and swollen flood hamper him at every step.

Silver is fifty per cent. premium here, and a small newspaper, printed by hand, in English, French and German, costs ten cents per copy.

The French quarter lies close to the terminus of the Canal, and, besides its neat dwellings, contains a park with a monument to Columbus grouped with an Indian maiden. This gives the origin of its usual name—Colon. Admiral Nelson is said to have spent a large part of one year here, when pursued by Napoleon Bonaparte and the French fleet.

One morning I took the Panama train en route for the Pacific coast, and rode from eight A. M. to early afternoon through the heart of the isthmus, of which we have heard so many fabulous tales from the early California miners. The orange and the jessamine were in full bloom. The cocoanut, mango, betelnut, banana and plantain grew in wild profusion on either side, and the bamboo and palm lent their thick jungle to enhance the view. Figuratively speaking, a dead body lies beneath each tie of the line. Hundreds of lives were sacrificed to the fatal fever during the construction of the road, and $500,000 spent in one of its bridges over the Chagres river. Even to-day the ties are of lignum vitae, and cost from three to five dollars apiece. No other wood will withstand the climate. The Jamaica negro, the Chinaman, and the native Indian, manage to exist, but the latter alone appears to take comfort, and that possibly because social life is not too exacting, and his children can bask at will in the birth-given robes of nature, and can earn their living by merely an outstretching of the hand. Numerous little and lean

ON THE SOUTH BANK OF THE PANAMA CANAL.

black hogs peer out of the bamboo huts. Contrasted with the children, they are quite neat and clean. This railroad was located by Col. Hughes and Totten of New York, and was incorporated at that place in 1849, but before completion the floods made such havoc that pretty much all of it had to be repaired. It was not possible to open it until 1855. Five thousand men and $7,500,000 were required. Vanderbilt at the same time opened his Nicaraguan route.

When the discovery of gold in California was made, thousands from the East flocked thither,—some overland, and thousands around perilous Cape Horn. Besides sailing vessels, there were a few steamers, such as the North America, which was seized by starving hundreds shipwrecked near Panama, and which was lost near shore, leaving her sick and discouraged passengers on that inhospitable shore to die like sheep. Just as their last hope was expiring, I am told, the S.S. Lewis, from around the Horn, with assistance and provisions, hove in sight, and rescued them from total destruction.

When the railroad opened, everything was changed. The long, perilous journey around the Horn was superseded by an easy and speedy trip by rail for about forty-nine miles through a tropical paradise. It is true the ship fever was less fatal than the fever of the isthmus, yet the exposure was so slight that comparatively few died therefrom. It is equally true that many preferred to walk across to paying a fare of $50 to $75 then asked for what we now get for but $5. The usual steerage passage from San Francisco to New York in those days was $150, and often more, and there were often so many applicants for berths that $450 in gold were sometimes given for another's ticket.

But to go on. While riding like Jehu, we saw an old Spanish castle and cathedral on our right, and a long line of pelicans disappearing over some water. Almost at the same time, Panama was announced. This place, with its orange tree streets and steep hills, is more strange than Aspinwall. Under advice of our physician, we spent only a day viewing its old curiosities and ruins, for the people were dying on every hand. We went over to the large island owned by the Panama railroad, and aboard the U. S. man-of-war, until we could get a steamer for Callao. The southern terminus of the canal is just over the bluff north of Panama and opposite our Marine burial ground, called Dead Man's Island. The snow-clad Cordilleras of South America loomed up on our left, with the old ivy and shrub-mantled cathedral in front. Long lines of dreamy looking pelicans rose and fell on the air, never failing in their unerring dives into the smooth sea to bring up a coveted fish. From the officers of the man-of-war Juniata, I ascertained that King Kalakaua of the Sandwich Islands, was besieged in his palace; that Queen Kapiolani was fast hastening home from her tour in the States, and, although our navy department had ordered two of our men-of-war to immediately start for Honolulu, it was decidedly unwise to visit the place. So I reluctantly, and for the first and only time during my long journey, abandoned my plan of travel.

I was within 7° of the equator, and knowing my course through Java and Sumatra would be below that circle, I determined to visit further South here; so, bidding adieu to the peaceful quiet, the long line of Jamaica negroes lustily pulling the oar, and sending their happy chorus over land and sea, we stood out to sea once more. On our right was the island from which alone drinking water was obtainable; on our left the rich, yet unproductive mountains of the United States of Columbia, while the fast-setting sun, with regal splendor, outlined our course over the placid Pacific. What moral power is felt at sea! The waking day, the rosy, rising sun stirs the heart to hopes and life; but at night its last lingering glance falls like a fond mother's gaze on her parting son.

Callao, as is well known, is the port of Peru, and its capital, Lima, and presents quite an animated scene. The United States man-of-war Alert lay at anchor, ready for action. As on the Isthmus, Spanish is the common language, and the Chinese the common laborer and trader. Little girls and boys of native mothers and Chinese fathers are often seen, as lovely as the stars, but shockingly disfigured by shears and the razor as soon as a trip to the Flowery Kingdom is contemplated.

CHAPTER III.

Where Spanish galleons roved of old.

From the time of Balboa to Magellan, doubtless, the immense expanse of water between Asia and America no more deserved its well-earned reputation for quiet and peacefulness than now, though the latter discoverer claims to have promulgated this attribute by giving it the name of the Pacific. Pacific it is in fair weather, it is true, but let the typhoon rise in its might, or the Sierra Madre mountain wind tear along its surface, and you begin to regard the name as a capital piece of irony, or those old voyagers a deceiving set of scoundrels. At Panama the tide rises thirty feet, greatly in excess of the Caribbean Sea, at the other end of the Canal, and, although the French have been dredging for three years there is little to show for it; another evidence is the many forlorn, stranded vessels you meet everywhere on the coast up to San Francisco. The fact is, take the Pacific at any point in the same latitude with the Atlantic, and you will have to catch it if you are out. A few days later I set out for the Central American states, through a sea like oil, huge sea turtles sleeping on the surface, and sea serpents winding their way among and over them, as on land. For days, as far as the eye could reach, if there was any departure from this thick fluid, it was but a gentle swell of pretty much the same appearance. What monotony! What *ennui!*

But one noon, when it had been so hot that we all had hardly anything but a backbone left, away in the distance we discovered what appeared a large ship coming down upon us as in a mirage. The snow-white foam was leaping up from her cutwater, and lo! a squall, wind, rain and hail poured in upon us from all directions. The awning over deck was snatched from over our heads with a boom like a cannon, and, in one short half hour, we were driven to overcoat and gloves. Dear, calm, old mother ocean, why practise the wily arts of a young woman! I must not forget to state that the apparent vessel was a death-dealing water spout, which proved too far to starboard to cause our ruin. After we could look about, we saw with joy the City of Panama, one of the Pacific mail steamers, alongside, bound for Acapulco, Mexico, which we signalled. She was a smaller and faster boat, and was far in advance by the next morning. When the elements rested on their arms we saw the high peaks of Costa Rica, the most southern of Central American republics, towering up on our right, and apparently ice streams running down their summits. Ice was $90 a ton on the Isthmus, and all along the coast to Southern California it never fell below $40, while in most places it was $60, which I afterwards found to be the price in Singapore and the East Indies.

The soil of Costa Rica is red, and contains rich deposits of gold, silver and antimony, while on every hand miles of valuable timber greet the eye, down to the water's edge, primeval groves, trackless forests, and only 3500 miles from San Francisco, less than half that distance from Acapulco, which should be connected with Mexico City and the Mexican Central railroad just as soon as circumstances will allow. The sea became as wavy as in a shower, and Spanish mackerel and porpoise leaped up on every hand, followed by the ugly dorsal fin of the shark slowly cutting through the glassy surface. We here met two steamers and passed two. Turri Alba, 12,500 feet, and Chiriqui, 11,265 feet high, both volcanos, appear, with Los Votos, 9,800 feet above us all. In close company of an ideal thunder storm, we steamed into the pretty bay of Punta Arenas. It has a beautiful beach and rolling surf; but this port, like all on the Pacific coast up to California, affords no wharfage for large steamers. All goods as well as passengers are conveyed to land in small boats or lighters.

We found coffee, sugar, cocoa, sarsaparilla, oranges, bananas and other freight, awaiting us, and we took the opportunity to see the country. For three dollars we secured a native boat, and, after running into and carrying away the line of two young ladies too intent on fishing to notice that they had unwittingly become fishers of men, were rapidly rowed to a high iron pier. It had a covering of like material, the only thing that is safe from the sea-worms. We were soon out on the smooth beach, which was so free from rock, stone or pebble, as to seem ground in a mortar. It was the Sabbath, and an old, but silvery chime was ringing the devout Catholic to service. The prevailing language is Spanish, so I was not surprised to find the religion Catholic. In fact, all through Central America and Mexico, I found this to be true. We walked from the beach up to a wide avenue shaded with orange trees laden with fruit, by open houses, with goods and fruit exposed for sale,—long strips of beef sun-dried and sold by the yard, side by side with Panama hats, selling from five to ninety dollars apiece; sugar in large cakes as dark as its owner, cheese as white as the lace of the plump, half-dressed maidens gliding about, and flowers rivalling all else in their splendor and fragrance. But cost, do not speak of it! It is the common impression that everything is given away in the tropics. If you have that impression still, stay at home, for, although one receives many a little tribute of unsophisticated nature from the people, the foreigner is generally regarded as a bonanza.

I need not stop to explain. A button hole bouquet costs fifty cents, my friend. Stay at home if you wish to travel and not pay dearly for it. Yes, stay at home. The houses are one-story, with tile roofs, and no chimneys or glass windows. As in all the tropics, iron window bars serve to keep out the lawless. Long rows of cactus hedge separate the lots, and make an impenetrable barrier. Buzzards were on the house tops, in the streets and under foot, and to kick one of the ugly pests would call down the ire of the whole town, for they are so necessary to the health of the country, so useful in destroying insect and reptile, they are become almost sacred. But ugh, the nasty birds.!

Long lines of covered two-wheeled ox-carts toiled into the town, with hides, tallow, copper, sugar and fruit, each drawn by two or three yoke of cattle, the only beast of burden. There was, however, a short line of railway building, by Northern men, to expedite commerce, but so short as to be of no great importance. Monkeys and parrots filled your eyes with laughter and your ears with confusion; and to step out into the woods was to make the acquaintance of the American leopard, bear and lion, the skins of which hung exposed on every dwelling. It is unfair to pass by this place without speaking words of praise for the women, and yet, words but ill express either admiration or appreciation.

The native Indian, and the mixed Spanish and native resemble the majority of Mexicans in dress, manners and personal appearance. The native is slim and graceful, the Mestiza plump, lovely and womanly, both of which classes, simply dressed in white, with ornaments of taste, impress one with a sense of genuineness that her Northern sister rarely can. It seemed to be but the outward manifestation of a pure, true soul, fresh from the hand of God, very like the beauty and fragrance of a flower; and ever afterward I found in the tropics the same fragrant and spontaneous purity of life, that put to shame higher civilization, and proved it selfish and cruel. The fare to San Francisco from here is $90 in gold.

Reluctantly bidding adieu, we left the beautiful bay with the sun, and steamed slowly into the Pacific. The next morning we were out of sight of land, and in the midst of Nature's celebration of thunder and lightning. The stars and stripes floating at the masthead received the ovation as peculiarly their own, for it was the glorious "Fourth of July." Before noon thirteen different nationalities were gleefully exploding fire crackers, torpedoes and jokes. After songs and games in the saloon, it was found that there was on board an Italian with a hand organ and little girl. After collecting ten dollars for a bribe, we prevailed on him to give an entertainment. The rigging was full of monkeys and pet birds, and we soon held such a carnival that would have dumbfounded the natives themselves. The organ proved treacherous, and from time to time would refuse to sing, though the Italian anxiously increased the speed of the crank, until it seemed impossible for the machine to hold together. A medical friend undertook to doctor it, but with as little success as on some of his patients, for, although none of the little painful stoppages longer occurred, no sooner did it approach the end of a bar than it ran screeching up into a high falsetto, or a laughable zip, zip, zip, that frightened the monkey, saddened the girl, and quite dismayed the "Duke" himself.

But it was a happy celebration in spite of the thoughts of far distant friends at home. The only occurrence to mar the pleasure was the slaughter on deck of an ox, as was the custom and need once in two days. All large steamers on the mid-Pacific carry oxen, sheep, swine and poultry, to kill for fresh food. The noble animal was led out from its pen by a strong rope fastened to its horns and made fast to the windlass of the donkey engine, and when the butcher, with bare arms and head, had finished whetting his murderous blade, he gave the signal for the engine to start, and to gradually drag the poor beast to its knees. Lowing with fright, it sank down, scattering everything within reach in its furious struggles to escape. This had once happened on the voyage, to the injury of many and the loss of one life. Lower and lower sank the head, when, darting forward, the butcher thrust his knife straight down behind the horns, and with a loud groan, the mighty beast fell over dyed in gore. In a trice the hide was off the quivering flesh, and the body hanging to the halliards.

How unhappy the thought that the life of man depends on taking the life of others! We seldom think of the vegetable, but how rarely of the poor brute! If you do this, can you blame the poor shipwrecked mariner for thirsting for the blood and flesh of his weaker comrade? Or is it a joy to the brute to die! Not far from this is the modern fabric of society. Those who have no thought or fear of punishment, drive rough shod over their suffering fellows, little thinking that might is not right, and that even on the morrow a day of reckoning may come.

But to return. A large right whale came alongside and threw up torrents of water while blowing, as if joining in our festivity. After our tea we disrobed our gaily-dressed spars and rigging of their bunting and streamers, and made the upper air alive with Roman candles and sky rockets; but, as if in sport, the mighty elements of wind and water swept down upon us, and furnished our startled eyes with so vivid and frightful a display of Nature's own pyrotechnics that we felt cheap and insignificant.

The next day we dropped anchor off the town of Libertad in San Salvador, which lies low with high peaks of volcanic origin in the background, one of which, north of Dos Hermanos, is particularly attractive both in height and outline. We found the capital of the republic twelve miles inland and of the same name, San Salvador. The national flag is not very unlike ours, as is the case with all these little republics. Indigo, an uncommon product in America, is largely grown, and balsam is also an export. The place has its barracks, but no formidable soldiery. The president was once obliged to come aboard and stay till an insurrection had been quelled. The surf is high and grand, the coast resembling that of Nantasket.

While viewing the background the first morning, my glass nearly fell from my hands as I saw in the distance the long-desired flash and puff of a living volcano. It sent up a long coil of smoke every fifteen minutes by my watch, which rose and disappeared, only to be followed by another and another. I had watched Vesuvius and other smaller elevations, but they had refused all entreaty or threats to exhibit; so to see, after many years, this clock-work regularity of volcanic action, was as novel and unexpected as it was grand. I saw further North, and in Japan, fully as interesting exhibits of power and grandeur, however. The steamer South Carolina, once used in the Rebellion, I believe, as a war vessel, steamed up, around, and away again without stopping. There came two-wheeled covered carts, drawn by yokes of patient oxen, slowly rolling down the trail to the town. Here, as in Southern Asia, sticks or pieces of bamboo are used in place of figures for counting.

After finding nothing new in the people, we set sail again for Acajutla, also in San Salvador. The coast is unlike that South, being low lying instead of ranges of steep hills or mountains, although high peaks loom up in the far distant interior. The volcano Izalcho was constantly in sight. There is a fine sandy beach and prettily curving bay. We found, also, interesting relics of green stone, and an old ruin on the plain outside of the town. We frequently, on our journey, found what appeared to be Aztec ruins—arches, columns, altars, and little stone images, but got no satisfactory account of their origin. The houses resemble those in Southern United States, and look more inviting than at any point yet reached.

From Acajutla we set sail for San Jose, Guatemala, which surpasses even Naples in the beauty of its bay and surrounding peaks. Long lines of surf were rolling in upon a wide, smooth beach, filling the ear with nature's choicest music. Birds of brilliant plumage flitted through the thick foliage, and were it not for the few dwellings and storehouses near the wharves, the scene would have been of primæval grandeur and simplicity. Several of the dwellings were two-storied, each story having its cool veranda. Away back in the distance rose two clearly cut peaks hiding their heads in the clouds, and further south, forming a symmetrical valley, rose another conical giant, so beautiful in its proportions and outline, I recall, in all my trip, no rival, except perhaps, Fusiyama in Eastern Japan. One of the pair of mountains is the volcano De Fuego, which, some years ago, suddenly broke out and destroyed Antigua, the old capital at its foot.

The new capital is on a plain some twenty miles inland, which we found connected by rail, so we were spared the fatigue of a ride in the saddle. Like all things of beauty and attractiveness, its superiority is offset by insuperable difficulties to pleasant enjoyment. Earthquakes, as well as volcanic eruptions, keep the Republic in a state of chronic uneasiness. Mould and decay attack and destroy leather and cloth in a most discouraging manner, and the centipede and scorpion are frequent, although unbidden, guests. Nor is it pleasant to have one side of your face in the possession of a gigantic tarantula. Yet the rare birds, species of wood and timber, not to omit the fertility of the soil, in part compensate for these dangers and discomforts, and farm houses are going up everywhere, and modern machinery coming fast into use. Sugar, coffee, and timber are the chief exports. For forty miles the fine beach extends northward, giving the native a natural and easy road to the seaport. Although one misses a high degree of intelligence in the people, fair mechanical skill is disclosed in their artistic pottery.

In my rambles through the country, two strange but

interesting sights surprised me,—one away from the haunts of man, the other under his full protection. In a thicket seldom visited, except by reptiles and wild beasts, I one day met the rare and beautiful national bird of the Republic. It is so shy that the eye of man rarely catches but a glimpse. There it perched, in its black, green and gold, with a body and beak like a parrot, and three long feathers floating down with all the colors of the rainbow to the extent of from three to four feet. The other experience was far from wild woods and in a place of safety, and although I had often observed a murderous-looking knife and a brace of revolvers decorating the waist of the people, I started when, one morning, I was accosted in Spanish by a soft feminine voice, and beheld a lovely, dark-eyed maiden, with rich olive complexion and long silk eyelashes, standing like a picture straight from the canvas, close at my side. A simple string of white pearls clasped her throat, relieved by her pure complexion on one side and a border of rare lace on the other, her slight, graceful form enveloped in a robe of fleecy texture and whiteness. She almost took my breath away. As with the macaw in the thicket, my first impression was of beauty, but a second glance revealed a revolver nestling amid the lace of her belt, and from her graceful shoulders a carbine hanging, a book of poems and a nosegay in her hand, and all sense of loveliness suddenly changed to wonder.

As nothing is farther from my object than to be sensational, I omit my personal experiences, and also the private history of those I meet. I merely note this peculiar experience as being not so very uncommon in countries of so unstable a government as Guatemala and other places in its neighborhood. This isolated, refined woman, transformed by force of necessity into an Amazon, possessed a firm little chin indicative of adequate ability to protect others also. In fact, I might give several pointed illustrations of this.

At last, I took steamer for Champerico, Guatemala, but on account of the high surf, rolling and pitching us about, we were obliged to wait amid its hollow roar and sublime beauty until the next morning before we could get out of the bay. Champerico boasts of one large two-story house with a cupola, a sight I had not seen for weeks if not months, a wharf, and a few well-constructed houses in its neighborhood, with a group of native thatched huts in the distance. Five high peaks are in full view, one inland, that of an active volcano. Mile after mile of wide, sandy beach stretches out before one with heavy growth of timber on its upper border. Both rice and the cocoanut palm would flourish, and yield large returns on such soil as is found here.

Our vessel rode so high that, in disembarking, use had to be made of a saloon chair, raised and lowered by the donkey engine. The sensation of spinning around was far from pleasant, to say nothing of rising high in the air, swinging out over the water in oscillation like an unsteady pendulum, and then descending with forty million jerks, each enough to send your heart into your mouth. Some native women, half Indian and half Spanish, left us here, much to my regret, as in my leisure moments I never tired of studying them. Northern Guatemala differs very little from the Southern. Sixteen hundred bags of coffee and sugar were carried aboard the vessel for the North, but I found a great want of capital and need of modern machinery everywhere.

When ready, I left for Acapulco, the oldest Western port in Mexico, 480 miles distant. The time may come when a line of railway may run the entire length of the Pacific Coast, but at the time I am writing, railroads are almost entirely unknown. Not even is Acapulco connected with the capital of Mexico, and eight days of steady riding is required for that journey. Travel by water gives its own peculiar pleasure, however, and in the warm season is in every way preferable. The steamer was a miniature forest. Monkeys swung from the rigging on every side, parrots laughed and scolded from nook and corner, and squirrels leaped and chattered from morning till night. Monkeys are bought for $3 apiece, parrots from $5 to $8, and squirrels, amadillos and other animals, from fifty cents upward. The squirrel resembles the grey of the North, but differs in being of a brown color.

Groups of thatched huts were distinguished, now and then, along the coast, indicative of a denser population than below. The Pacific at once assumed its glassy and viscous appearance, and at night fifty large sea turtles, at one time, appeared basking upon its surface. As darkness set in we seemed to be ploughing through molten silver, so wide did the disturbed water throw up its sparkling phosphorescence. It was sultry even on deck, and we remained up drinking in the calm still night and the brilliant scintillations both of sea and sky, when suddenly out of the ominous stillness, from the Northeast, no larger than a man's hand sprang a halo. Down upon our weary heads burst a cold, icy wind that struck to the marrow. Up and down, in and out, it raged, tearing away our awnings, snapping out stays and bombarding our vessel with gigantic waves, till all thought or desire of sleep quite vanished.

Now sitting up on her stern, like a water fowl flapping her wings, and now lying sheer over on her side, as if to take a complete roll, our gallant vessel wrestled with the now thoroughly enraged deep. I knew now we had reached the Gulf of Tehauntepec. All the following day it continued, but with some abatement. I had never had so rough an experience but once—that was when within two days' sail of Queenstown, while going abroad for study, just after leaving college. But that was the Atlantic. It had not the power to deceive. What a commentary on the appropriateness of the term Pacific! Yet let me say that I enjoyed those two days and nights, in their freedom from monotony, from heat and from laziness, more than any on the coast. We soon came in sight of the distant Sierra Madre del Sud, an unbroken, ragged chain of mountains in Southwestern Mexico, which seemed to never leave us until we reached port, and to come down to the very coast with its high border of rock. The sea became like oil again.

We stood off a pretty little harbor with thatched roofs peering up now and then, and near an island with a light house on our port. Not far distant another island rose, on which, with my glass, an old Spanish fort was discernible. Other islands running up to sharp peaks appeared scattered along until we suddenly dropped anchor before a low coast, with barren hills on the north and high mountains in the distance. Away in the distance I descried palms, bananas and large lime trees shading a paved way to an old stone fort. I could see soldiers pacing up and down, though both fort and guard looked as though it had seen no mortal since the time of Noah. The hull of the old Moses Taylor, of fragrant memory to old forty-niners, lay like the skeleton of a camel in a desert, high on the beach. It is now passed by with but a glance, yet what joy, what sadness, what conflict within and without, what despair has met the human soul on that old vessel! Not far distant the Alaska, of the Pacific mail, also lies abandoned. Near, the San Jose is loading. Noble cocoanut palms loom up everywhere down to the water's edge. Securing a native boat we were rowed ashore, and guided up the half paved way to the entrance of the fort, stopping only to speak with the little children and women coming from their adobe houses by the wayside, and finding an officer on duty, received a polite invitation to enter.

Over a well at the western side, a well so ancient and odd looking, that one would be forgiven did he imagine that Rebecca must have once sat here, is a large tablet in the wall, on which I, after a long study, made out the figures 1608 cut therein, but so worn by the weather as to be hardly legible. The whole structure is brown, and crumbling with age, has an old-fashioned moat and long slits in the walls for arrow or rifle. A mere handful of men, hardly a full company, garrisoned it, but they might in one week fall an easy prey to as many of their mosquitoes. They were short, slim and weak, something like Uncle Sam's regulars on the frontier. The officer wore a green plume on his wide-brimmed hat, but nothing else, except his sword, distinguished him from his comrades. However, his graciousness is to be commended.

Out over the town we went, cocoanuts, bananas, aligator pears and flowers everywhere. Neat little houses of white and blue, disclosing at a glance the whole interior with hammock and brass bedsteads, and quiet, cool courts in the rear, full of bright birds, vines and flowers, lined the neat but narrow streets. Children, surprised by our advance, ran swiftly away, while man, woman and child flocked to their doorways and iron-latticed window openings, to watch our every movement. For some distance up the steep hill on the north are built stone basins, so that the water from above runs from one to another until all are full. All have to go there for drinking, washing and cooking purposes, and lucky is the lad that, too lazy to dip out the fluid and perform his laundry work in his own proper vessel, completes his toil — and his toilet at the same time — and escapes out of said wells without discovery. But woe appeareth on the face of the next comer.

At the foot of the lowest of these stone wells we came upon a party of boys lazily at work in the hot sun, dressing swine. Many a poor little black porker lay flat on its side, with its hair partly removed, and left to spoil in the sun, while the youngsters splashed about in the drinking water above. We were thirsty and tired. Some stepped forward and took up the ladle for a draught. Their hands fell spasmodically to their side. They stared around as if in search of a gun. Women offered us fruit and flowers plucked before our eyes. Next to the flowers, in beauty and fragrance, came the women and children, but for fear that my object may be misconstrued, I will not descant upon their many charms.

Up across the ancient plaza, with its old well and rare trees, we entered the old cathedral, over the doors of which is inscribed a text in Latin. We were received by the swell of a distant organ and the voices of the choir softly chanting vespers. Little girls with strings of pretty white shell necklaces besought us to buy, and choir boys approached to solicit alms for the church. In the rear is an old vine-mantled bell-tower which speaks of the early Spanish.

For many a year those old Spanish buccaneers and adventurers sailed up to this port on their way to and from Mexico, and my curiosity was excited to see the old trail used from time immemorial over this course. Has my reader ever seen a burro? Does he know whether he walks on his feet or hops on his head? If he does, he knows more than I could learn in this wild, forsaken country. My companion was some six and a half feet in height, and wore a hat that had a rim that threw Aunt Keziah's gingham umbrella quite into the shade. Mounted on one of those eccentric little quadrupeds, with his feet drawn up to prevent their dragging on the rough ground, a knife and a brace of old-fashioned pistols sticking up from his narrow waist, and his sombrero lamely flapping in the breeze, he looked with surprise that I should see anything comical in our situation or appearance.

Ah, well, those were halcyon days, and I will not spoil any reader's chances of sport or revelation by disclosing the possibilities of a personal experience. I will say, however, that we saw the trail—and much of the surrounding ground. If Dickey interrupted an earnest conversation by wickedly assuming a perpendicular, or broke in upon our ecstatic contemplation of a distant landscape, with a startling roar and sudden activity of hind heels, it was nothing amusing; of course not. Only a bare fact—and often a bare head and elbow. The treasured rosewood cane, with which I had been presented by a planter in Guatemala, stood me in good use, as a gentle reminder to the vixen, that I, and not he, was to be the rider.

I used to read with wonder how the angel of the Lord met Balaam on the highway, seated upon some such a steed as this, and how the beast spoke right out. I feel convinced that poor Balaam's experience was, more than once, my own, except there was no vision from heaven to declare to my bewildered mind whether the braying beast was really talking or singing.

On the return down the mountains to the town, the view was grand beyond description. The quiet hour of evening, the sinking sun, and the flood of silvery music from the chimes below, will never be forgotten.

The castle of San Diego, the land-locked harbor, with its shipping like huge birds upon its quiet surface, rise in memory like a dream.

Acapulco was the great depot for Spain in her early commerce with Manilla and the East Indies. Once a year a galleon set out for that place, and one returned. On its arrival here, a great fair was held, attended by merchants from all parts of Mexico. Since that time it has been overthrown by numerous earthquakes, but it still is one of the important seaports of Mexico, and exports vanilla, cocoa, indigo, cochineal, wool, and hides, and exceeds 5,000 in population. Its connection with the overthrow and capture of the unhappy Maximilian is too well known to repeat. The food is the same as in use throughout Mexico: tortillas made of grain, ground by the women between stone rolling-pin and tablet, eggs, frijoles, and fruit. The people are not so neat as desirable, yet the middle and upper classes compare favorably with New Englanders, both in personal appearance and courtesy towards strangers. The natives, in rude dugouts, surrounded our steamer, and patiently awaited our patronage for such fruits and merchandise as they exposed for sale. The least misstep or haste with the paddle sent them, goods and all, deep into the water. No such scene as Bret Harte describes now presents itself to the eye:

> "In sixteen hundred and forty-one,
> The regular yearly galleon,

> Laden with odorous gums and spice,
> India cotton and India rice,
> And the richest silks of far Cathay,
> Was due at Acapulco Bay."

Needing fresh meat, we took on board half a dozen bullocks, by fastening a rope about the horns and running it over the yard-arm and attaching it to the drum of the donkey-engine. Slowly starts the engine, tightening the rope and gradually raising the animal's head and forequarters. It soon stands on hind tiptoe, then off swings the helpless beast into mid-air. Not a groan, not a struggle, and when carried high aloft and gently let down to deck, no sign of life, except a weak struggle to rise. I wondered at this. The next day, when out on the broad ocean again, I accidentally found out the cause of all this want of animal vigor. Right before me and the sun, hung the huge dressed carcass of one of these poor brutes. I could see nothing but bones and a thin skin—call it flesh if you will—red and transparent, uniting the same. In fact, the animals were cactus fed, and those of you who have wandered over many a weary mile of parched country and found nothing but thistles, can appreciate the situation.

Without recounting other Mexican experiences and places, I will merely mention the port of Mazatlan, which is, on account of the mines, now a strong rival to Acapulco. After encountering a school of blackfish, and steering clear of a water-spout, we ran into a frightful thunder and lightning storm, which, however, left us unharmed, and the sea as smooth as glass. It was on the first day out that I read in the Mexican newspapers that the Panama Canal Company had at last succumbed to the inevitable. I need not say now that the news was incorrect, but every one on board believed it, so little faith had they that the French would succeed. The second day we nearly sank under another water-spout, but reached Manzanillo, which will soon be connected, it is hoped, by rail with all the large cities and towns in the centre of Mexico.

But to go on. I soon saw the volcano of Colima. The coast is dotted with fine, large islands of white rock. We passed Cape Corrientes at 3 P. M. that day, but at once stood out to sea again, with cloudy sky and pleasant but cool breeze. The sea at night was resplendent with scintillation, rivalling the milky way in splendor. Same day, passed Las Tres Morias. We were then on line with the Sandwich Islands. At night caught sight of the high telegraph station announcing our arrival at Mazatlan. High, abrupt precipices rose all around.

With full speed we turned into the channel, and gracefully curved up to a high rock as if to pierce it, and quickly cast anchor, bringing us up into close quarters with cacti and wild flowers on its bank. We must have been three miles from the town, but with the glass I discovered the high chimney of a mill, a garrison house, a pretty fortification, a corso, and an immense cathedral. At 9 P. M. the quarantine officer came aboard and put us to a rigid examination. The following morning we found that we had anchored right beneath the lighthouse, which is built like an old Moorish castle. The harbor was full of peaked islands. We sent on shore large quantities of mining machinery, some Alexandrian Turks, a Spanish gentleman from Santander, Spain, and took on two New England men.

The place had more shipping than Acapulco. Taking a boat, after a row of three or four miles, we were landed on the low coast and left to go where we pleased. The cathedral has been building for years, and is still unfinished. Northern men have established a match factory here, and one for making ice. The owner told me that his match business was a success, but that his ice machine, duty and all, had cost him $8,000, but, although he had large contracts for this delicacy, his machine, as at that very time, would get out of order and necessitate a trip of hundreds of miles to San Francisco to obtain the needed repairs. I also found a cotton mill and machine shop in full operation. It has a corso for bull fighting, a sport from which I kept away in disgust, although the horses and bulls engaged, it seemed to me, had not the strength to stand up before the blast of a pair of bellows.

What interested me, next to the people, was the specie, ore, and ingots of solid silver, constantly going aboard the steamer for San Francisco. The specie, in the form of Mexican dollars for China, was shipped in wooden casks, which were rolled up and down the deck of the small shore boat like kegs of nails. I doubt the natives knew the nature of their precious freight, for while the sea was sending both vessels up and down, away went one of the casks, worth from $1300 to $2000, and before it could be stopped, splash-dash into the sea. I was told, later, that the divers sent in search returned the report that no trace of it could be found. At the same time I was led to understand that, as soon as we had got under way, some fine night those very divers would go straight to the lucky spot, and ever after be a wonder to their countrymen and a source of envy to their neighbors in their display of horse trappings and denaro. It is difficult to describe the inordinate pride a Mexican takes in rigging out both himself and steed in solid silver and fringe. Hundreds of pesos are often squandered in this way, and paraded before a gaping crowd by many a vain and worthless caballero.

The ore is mostly shipped in wooden boxes, but sometimes in bags. It is a strange sight, but common if you ride out a hundred miles, to see a line of pack mules, in single file or in pairs, slowly plodding along a trail, a few soldiers on guard, and three large silver bricks, 12x6x6 inches, bulging out from side and back of the patient beast, which toils, now up, now down, the rocky steeps. It has no thought or knowledge of the preciousness of its burden or the danger its exposed and tempting appearance invites from the bold outlaw infesting the woods and ravines along its unprotected pathway. Mazatlan has always been celebrated for its black pearls, mineral wealth, not to say for its pirates and outlaws, but good government has of late much changed the place.

These bricks of solid silver were brought on board without a shadow of protection or covering, and deposited on the open deck under the feet of all. They resembled babbitt-metal or solder, according to the refinement, but it did not surprise me. The mind becomes so accustomed in the tropics, to gold, silver, precious stones, and all that is beautiful and fragrant, it would enter heaven here with such complacency as to astonish its Maker. Thirty-seven years has His house, the cathedral, been building, and is still unfinished.

When I boarded my steamer for San Francisco, I found fifteen different nationalities represented by its passengers. In conversation with the owner of the ice machine, before mentioned, he stated that he usually made two tons of ice daily, and sold it for $50 per ton, and that a mere hole in the piping, allowing the ether to escape, had not only prevented him from keeping his contract to supply steamers then in port, but had obliged him and his brother to take a three weeks' journey for repairs.

Soon after leaving the coast, when near Cape St. Lucas, the temperature fell again. It served, however, to relieve the parched, hot sands of lower California and its reddish hills. At the Cape is a pretty little arch and cave, with the billows rolling up and through, almost too inviting to pass by. North of it are miles of smooth, yellow sand, which appeared to be flowing down to the water's edge, giving the appearance of drifting snow. Passed Cape Tosco, with high peaks, followed by Margarita Island and Cape Lazaro. It still continued cold. Margarita Island, and Magdalena Bay, is where so many colonists died like sheep for want of water. It was here that Vanderbilt's S.S. Independence went to the bottom, wrecked by a sunken rock. Thousands of acres are in the possession of a San Francisco gentleman, who gathers its orchilla moss for purple dye. Water, in small quantities only, can be found, but even amid the hundreds of miles of barren sand hills and slopes, the native Indian, by instinct, will often point out a refreshing supply by merely scooping up the sand.

While speaking of the mining trains, I forgot to state that the average load allowed by the owner of a mule is about 300 pounds, for a burro 200, and that silver ingots usually weigh from 90 to 150 pounds apiece, so these are usually strapped to the pack-saddle, and although the load looks light and attractive, it really forms no small burden in this mountainous country. Taking into consideration that in many cases the government guard is made up of convicts, and that the government, not the convict, gets the pesos, it is not difficult to see the peculiar unhappiness and risk of the whole business.

The duties, too, are as great a source of loss and annoyance A young man I met in the mines told me that he bought a saddle in San Francisco for $40, and when he brought it ashore at Mazatlan he was obliged to pay a like sum for duty. Machinery is treated in the same way, and the diamond drill, and other improved machinery, is now considered indispensable to keep in advance of the native miners.

Now that I am leaving the unfrequented tropical countries, I would like to say something about their strange fruits and flowers, but it is so difficult to convey the sense of flavor or loveliness, I shall leave the subject to oblivion. The orange, banana, pine apple, cocoanut and sweet potato are common, in one form or another, to all; but the lime, tamarind, vanilla, cocoa, betel nut, yam, plantain, mango, guava, mammee and papaw apple, alligator pear, and many others, are to most of you unseen, if not quite unknown. There is a variety of banana called the fig banana which is also never seen North, but all these are as common here as the apple is at home. July 16, my diary states, was as cold as Greenland, though flying fish and the large bird called the booby were thick about us, and often overshot their mark and landed on deck, and soon became the prey of passenger and crew.

Black Warrior Lagoon, with the hills of Northern Lower California in full view, where seal fishing is carried on for oil, and the orchilla moss is gathered for dye, next appeared. Cedros Island, with the first trees we had seen for days, towering up here and there, and ravine-marked and gullied surface hardly fit for the wild goats we found thereon, followed. Acres of sea weed lay between island and coast, flashing up its varied color from its low ocean bed, many being fifteen and twenty feet in length and of rankest growth. Large islands covered with boobies, pelicans and ducks were in full view, revealing rich deposits of guano. Cedros Island contains the only fresh water for hundreds of miles, and a whaler lay alongside for a supply. Its shore presented a sad spectacle in rude wooden monuments placed over graves of seaman and whaler, either a victim of disease or anger of the mighty whale which swarms here to breed.

If there is anything attractive about the spot, next to whales and seals, it is seals and whales. Up pops the narrow head of a seal. Down flaps the frightful fluke of a whale. You like to see the monster of the deep afar off forcing up its cascades of foam, but the moment he begins to lash the surface in the majesty of his power, and protection of its young, then, somehow, you feel a strong preference for a seal, or wild goat, or even the land.

It was as cool as November in New England. The assistant rector of Trinity Church, New York, preached for us in the saloon the day before, and the cool temperature seemed to have awakened him from his customary inaction. We made San Diego, the oldest settlement in California, now soon to be the entry port of all the Speckels vessels from the Sandwich Islands. This may prove as great a rival to San Francisco in the South as, Victoria with its Canadian Pacific R. R., is in the North. It will receive the mails as well. Thousands of nautili, or Portuguese men-of-war, floated about our vessel, and acres of the yellowish white substance, known to seafaring men as whale food, stretched out before us, and we made Anaheim, Monica and Los Angeles. A three-masted schooner ran across our wake, the first sailing vessel in motion we had met for weeks. Passed between Santa Cruz and Santa Rosa at sun-down, in water 2,500 feet deep, and made Santa Barbara.

We soon saw Point Conception Light. The temperature was almost at the freezing point. The whole appearance of land and sea had changed, and, in spite of the cold, I was amused to hear one after another exclaim, "Thank heaven, we are in God's country again at last!" With the exception of two cattle ranches below San Diego, we had seen for days no sign of civilization, and when we now caught sight of Pedro Blanco Light, and ranches of wheat, alfalfa and cattle on the slopes of the Coast Range beyond, our joy knew no bounds. Off Monterey we discovered a new light-house going up. There is an old Spanish mission here of quaint and simple style, and many fine dwellings about a beautiful bay. Seals came in sight again, either elevating their peaked heads above the sea or sleeping quietly on the beach.

We had then reached the boisterous billows again, and soon were laboring through the rough current and sea of the Golden Horn with its bristling forts and earth-works to Telegraph Hill, and on to our dock. This was the first dock we had used for weeks, either on account of their absence or the shallowness of the harbor waters South. But what a sight met our eyes! In Eastern United States, July and hot weather are inseparable. In the same latitude East and for hundreds of miles North, people were sweltering in the heat, and longing for ice cream and lemonade, but here on the dock a young lady stood energetically waving a disengaged hand, and muffled from top to toe in sealskin. Her male companion, quietly puffing at a cigar, is as thoroughly encased in fur cap and ulster.

We felt a cool breeze creeping to our marrow. We were little prepared for landing in Washington and finding a Greenland. Here it was, however. Not a soul but what wore heavy winter clothing, and we but six days from a climate where it would have been burdensome to bear even a fig-leaf! This then was the much praised California climate! "But you will like it after you have spent a few days, and you can wear the same clothing the year round" they said. Bah! Ugh! Cliff House, park and seals, Chinatown, the Palace and other large hotels, were seen, few invitations out from my friends accepted, and then I left for Yosemite Valley and the Geysers, in wonder that so many poor wretches were living under the impression that they enjoyed an unusually fine climate.

To be just, I found upon reaching Oakland, six miles southeast, that San Francisco was alone in its execrable summer climate. During the remainder of my Californian trip the weather was as soft and mild, and the sky as clear as in Italy, and beyond anything I had experienced at home in New England. The Sacramento River, however, is a dirty, shallow stream with no public crossing until you reach South Vallejo, where a small steamer with petroleum engines—since destroyed by explosion—takes you over to the town. Mares Island is the United States Navy Yard and Hospital. Here I saw once more Farragut's old flagship, the Hartford. Napa, the home of Eustes, and the seat of one of the finest and largest insane hospitals in the world; Helena, surrounded by hundreds of acres of vine and fruit orchards; Cloverdale, with its petrified forests, were in turn visited, and other places in Napa, Sonoma and Lake counties, the Bradford and Johnson mines, St. Helena volcano, and through the vast Sonoma Valley, where reaping machines propelled by eight strong horses were gathering and stacking the heavy wheat, with a precision and ease perfectly wonderful.

From valley to foot-hills on the very summit of the Coast Range, the vine has supplanted the pine and cedar, and strong, costly granite store houses meet one on every hand, and often built directly out into the road you are travelling. Up, up, up, as fast as brute strength and speed can carry you, and faster than is either safe or agreeable, you go, until your weary team are, from sheer exhaustion, forced to a walk. Then, perchance, down again through a little valley on a wild and dangerous gallop, which brings a wicked gleam into the eyes of the driver as he casts a furtive glance youward to see if it makes its due and desired impression, until off goes his hat, and, in clouds of dust and over-heated air, you, with a little pardonable malice, watch him striding back for its recovery. The driver was of Spanish birth, who, when young, ran away from his home in the Sandwich Islands, because his mother desired him to accompany her to California.

I will not weary you with the story of his capture,

return, and captivity until that State was finally reached. It, I believe, made him entertain a secret enmity towards the whole human race, and when later on this journey of 30 miles, he allowed his horses to run like mad down a rough ravine, I volunteered to advise that more careful driving would save his master's property, if not our lives. I need not say my efforts were of little service to his master, for, all at once, down went the right front axle, throwing him headlong over the horses. I happily landed in a soft spot with only a sprain or two. Would you have blamed me if I had talked loud of Lynch law and its sure consequences? But I did not. It was I, though, who, some two hours after, when he had walked back a mile or two, and traversed the same distance on his return, for means to repair the coach, became quite satisfied with everything, urged him to put his animals to greater speed, and pointedly reminded him of the worthlessness of human life in general, and his in particular.

Away scuttled the upland lizard, this way then that, attempting two ways at the same time. Wild birds flew screeching on before, and wild beasts slunk growling aside. Up, up, up, till the broad Pacific appeared but a mere irregular line in the far western horizon, and the rich Sonoma valley spread out in all its summer beauty, lay fast disappearing at our feet. Still up, up, up, away from cultivated field and habitation of man, until the breath comes quicker and faster, the pulse runs wild, and you bow before the majestic heights and distant valleys as to hallowed ground. No pen can paint the exhilaration, the grandeur or the silent power of mountain influence. Our path did not permit of surplus space. Down, down the steep inclines with walls of solid stone sheer to the sky on the left, and wild, overhanging precipices on the right, into which a misstep, a rolling stone or the slightest swerve would land our almost breathless bodies hundreds of feet on the jagged rocks below.

While thus whizzing along, we saw directly in our track a little mass of brown and white. Cupidity alone could have led our driver to suddenly check his coach. We also became interested, but before we could descend it suddenly bounded up and across to a thicket. Searching, we soon found a young deer, as graceful as a gazelle, hiding its pretty head in the leaves to escape, as it imagined, from the sight of its pursuers. There is something pathetic in the actions of the young, and animals are not exceptions, and when I afterwards saw this same little fawn by the side of a bright little mountain maiden, to whom it had been given, I felt grateful that it had fallen into little, gentle hands that could love and protect it. Yet, with the little fawn stowed away in the only available spot left in the coach, we still rolled on, swaying here and pitching there, down the zigzag way to deep chasms over which the eagle and buzzard crossed with but a few strokes of their broad wings, but which we avoided by narrow, fish-hook curves so sharp as to threaten, in our rash descent, to snap our vehicle in two.

There sat our Jehu, with one foot pressed with all his strength on brakes, and a firm yet half comical curve about his mouth, in still greater danger than his passengers. As the right wheels were taking a log which served to widen the rocky path to a sufficient width to admit of crossing, there came a sickening swish, a jerk and a thud. We thought our last day had come, but happily not we found, for the wheels had merely slipped from the log to a crevice and sunk to the hub, holding the coach like a vice. Had the log been anything but one of those immense mountain trees, it would have been carried away with our momentum. We at last picked ourselves up and helped extricate the carriage. Going back a little, the lower part of the wheels could be seen hanging over the awful chasm, the bottom of which we could not discern, and wedged in so firmly that the prospect of seeing volcanoes or geysers seemed, to say the least, indefinitely postponed. For the first time our driver showed some signs of humanity, by confessing that his team was new and hard bitted, but that he thought it was as good an occasion as any to break them in, a disclosure calculated, as you can imagine, to add little to our mental peace.

But I will pass swiftly over these mountain experiences, the trails of wild beast, the lonely clearing with its sweet, bright-eyed children, so like a country home in the East, where the arrival of the letter or newspaper we brought, was the event of the month, perhaps the year. I could see how gently their little hands clasped around it, as they all fell into one embrace, and were left by us standing with clasped hands and rapt, upturned faces. Ah, how many times we feel the sweet simplicity of that country life! He has never lived who has not known the country — the song of birds, the fragrance of flowers, the hush of the forest unconsciously soften the heart, quicken the imagination and fill the soul with God's choicest emotions.

In these mountain fastnesses, the deer, the trout and the robin met us everywhere, even where the throbbing ground grew too hot for human feet, and fiery steam burst out dangerously upon us. Geysers are usually indicated at a distance by a strong odor of sulphur and long lines of yellowish-white deposit on the surface of the ground. Then follow springs of sulphur, magnesia, alum and other minerals, side by side, cold and hot, so as to boil an egg in a few minutes and cool it in five by just changing your hand. The heights of spray and steam are not usually uniform or regular. They may burst suddenly before your astonished gaze, hurling stones and other debris like canister shot, scorching your face and hands, if not blistering your whole body. Then, again, there may be but a rumble, a puff and irregular breathing from the vent holes. Fine enough curiosities to visit, but very objectionable neighbors and resting-places. Two days and one night sufficed in my case.

To speak of Yosemite Valley, Mariposa and Calaveras, awakens too many pleasant memories to jot down here anything but the merest outline. The last two have nothing of paramount interest except their cedars or redwood trees. It is not difficult to find them fifteen feet in diameter and from one to two hundred feet in height. In Mariposa Grove, via Berenda, there are fifteen of these trees, running up almost to the top without any considerable branches, measuring from 60 to 90 feet in circumference, and over 300 feet in height. A coach and six horses passes daily through the trunk of one of these, without grazing the sides, and leaving sufficiently firm walls to support and nourish the remainder of the giant. Among those of Calaveras, the Father of the Forest, now prostrate, is 435 feet long and 110 feet in circumference, and has rings disclosing an age of 3,000 years or more. The largest now standing is called the Mother of the Forest, and is 321 feet high and 90 feet at its base. They belong to the taxodium family, and are called Sequoia, after a Cherokee chief of that name.

Yosemite Valley is 4,000 feet above sea level, and

has the Merced river running southwesterly through it. In many places its walls are nearly vertical and add 4,000 feet for the surrounding mountains. The Bridal Veil, Yosemite, and Virgin Tears Falls on either hand make you stand speechless in wonder and delight. Point Inspiration, as you enter the valley, looms up like a giant sentinel, while for the whole nine miles of its length grateful surprises await and spring upon you when little expected. At the upper end you meet the Vernal Falls and Mirror Lake, a pretty little sheet of water, reminding one of Switzerland. Mt. Starr King is seen just south of these; and Sentinel Dome, from which the best view is obtained, lies a little further southwest. But, still having 25,000 or more miles to make, taking Southern California with its sandy plains, irrigated hills and valleys, its fruit and flowers into my eager vision the best I might, I hastened back to San Francisco. Every one seemed a real-estate broker and to live by doing just what the New Testament claims caused the death of Ananias and Sapphira. Comment is unnecessary.

On my return to San Francisco, I found the climate still unbearable. I entered a Market Street cable car, with dust from a sixteenth to an eighth of an inch deep on hat and shoulders, but before reaching my hotel, the rampant wind had removed nearly every particle of it.

I took passage for Japan on one of the finest

Pacific steamships ever engaged in the Eastern trade, and soon was off the Cliff House, with its old one-eyed seal and companion, and in the very jaws of Golden Gate, which, although it seems but a few hundred feet in width, is in reality a mile and a half. To my surprise and great pleasure, I found a young Spanish gentleman going to Manilla, with whom I had a pleasant acquaintance, was to accompany me to Yokohama, as also were Bishop Warren and lady of Colorado, who were on their way to a church conference in Tokio.

A JAPANESE COIN.

CHAPTER IV.

Fast fades our native shore,
All friends behind, a trackless sea before.

Although we had from 300 to 400 Chinese on board, they only served to occupy my interested attention whenever they appeared on deck or in our way. I was glad to see that the stories, told by missionaries and clergymen, in regard to white passengers being obliged, for want of money, to live and sleep among the Mongolians, were no longer true. With the exception of two women and three girls from Peru, all of whom were connected with the Chinese in one way or another, I found no mixture of races. There was one man, however, whom I at first supposed to be an American, as he had no queue or obliquity of eye, but who, I found, was a tea merchant from Georgia, where he had married a planter's daughter, and who by his choice English and urbane manners, really appeared foreign to them all. I often fell into conversation with him, as he seemed to avoid his companions, and disclose no bad Chinese traits. However, just before we reached the first Chinese port, to my surprise, I found not only the narrow shoe and wide flapping trousers, but a respectable queue, which, with the aid of braided ribbon and tape, he had brought down quite to his heels. Knowing the treatment the poor fellow would have received on shore, among his kin and neighbors, and probably from his government, one quickly overlooked this apparent weakness. It was merely self-protection. Nor was his the only case of metamorphosis. Lovely little children with bright, happy faces, on the day for landing, timidly trudged along with shaved head and eyebrows, abashed and ashamed of the cruel disfigurement custom had thus perpetrated.

The entire crew were Chinese, but were officered by Americans. I soon learned that it was not solely on account of economy in the pay roll. One illustration will suffice. On our third day out, while making my customary turn on deck, I found directly at my feet what, at first sight, appeared like a queerly shaped log. It was some eight feet in length and about two feet wide. Its wider and upper surfaces were flattened, and the four edges, corresponding to those of an ordinary box, were deep grooves instead of sharp lines. There was no one near except the officer on the bridge, so I continued my investigation. That it was the work of human hands was clear, but for what purpose I could not imagine, until I at last discovered on the upper surface what resembled, more than anything else, last year's crow tracks. It was Chinese! Was it a trunk or bed? Then it flashed across my mind the possibility that its Chinese owner was lying cold and stiff somewhere within. On looking up, my eyes met those of the officer of the watch, which in a glance answered my inquiry.

Many a grief-stricken mother, in my presence, on the Atlantic, had been forced, even though but two or three days from her native land and home, to give to the cruel deep a little boy or girl, and in one case, in 1874, while we were within two days' sail of Great Britain, two little girls, who had crossed the United States from San Francisco, and had become listless and weary before taking the long sea voyage, became worse, and one, despite physician and mother, slowly closed its gentle eyes in the sleep that knows no waking. She was so lovely and bright, she had become our own, and yet before night, against our earnest entreaties, her little form, so peacefully sleeping, so like a pink gathered from the garden, dearer and more sweet than in life, was cast out into the pitiless sea.

It is but one of my past experiences, making the rule that an American receives an ocean burial before twenty-four hours after death; but here, right before me, lay the foreigner, the Chinese. What of him? For eighteen days and nights our steamer bore the remains of that Celestial, until his bones could find rest in his native country. Why? "Because," said the officer, "If we buried a Chinaman at sea, it would anger the whole nation, and the Chinese trade would be totally-ruined." Had I, had Bishop Warren died, before nightfall our remains, sewed up in a sail-cloth and weighted with a few pieces of old iron, would have been over the vessel's side, the prey of wave and shark.

From that day I closely studied the much-vexed Chinese question, and although an ocean steamer is not the best place for accurate and fair comparison, I found that all my observations were afterward confirmed by like experiences in their native land. The forward decks were set apart for these people, and for eighteen days it was impossible to get some of them out into the open air or on the hurricane deck without absolutely pulling them out by the hair of their heads. With but a very few exceptions they squatted or lay flat upon the floor or thin rush mats, gambling and smoking their vile opium. Only at meal time was the scene changed. Thousands of dollars changed hands, and, I am told, went in a large measure to professionals and stewards. No sight is more pitiable than to see the strained attitude, the glaring eye and frantic contortions of a Chinaman half crazed with greed or disappointment; nothing more beastly, more swinish, than men and women lying at full length, or curled up, in a cloud of sickening opium smoke, with glazed eyes and death-like features as unconscious of your presence as in the tomb. This was an every-day sight, and I found but one redeeming feature, that almost every one could read and write. But, as with all mental education, so called, if the heart be not at the same time enlightened, there is no certainty of moral sense or good manners.

The Hindoo, the Japanese, even the Malay, on meeting me on the street, politely stepped aside with an apologetic movement of the body or courteous lifting of the hand to head or breast. Not so the Mongolian of China. He has a stupid selfishness, that takes up the whole way and elbows even women and children aside. It was only at the cry of my sedan bearers, and from fear of bodily injury, that progress in their ten-foot streets could be made at all. The same want of courtesy was intensified to boldness, on the ocean.

The first two days, on a northwesterly course, the air was cold and the sea raging, but the next two days were quiet and enjoyable. We were followed by flocks of boobies and albatross, measuring from tip to tip, three feet or more. Hardly a day thereafter, until near Japan, were those tireless companions absent from our view. Hour after hour I have stood at the stern rail, while those giant birds, with steady eye and motionless wings, like birds of prey pursued. To this side of our wake then that, as regular as a pendulum, swung their onward flight. Suspended on their huge wings and propelled by the momentum of their heavy bodies, down they glided almost to the water's level, and nearly on their right side, on a curve that carried them gracefully into the high air again, only to be unceasingly repeated, until your wonder grew to a strange fascination. In all that long distance, but a few times did we catch them resting on the water, and then to quickly spread their wings, run a few steps on the sea, and off into the air again.

Our course lay far to the north, so that for days we met, on every hand, countless flocks from the Alaskan Islands. We were supposed to shorten our journey on such a circle, and come down upon Japan with an advantage over the Canadian line, but the ocean was three times in ten days stirred up by fierce typhoons that caused unusually long and strong coast currents. These set in directly against us, so that often with full steam we made but little actual progress. To one experiencing one of these frightful revolving storms for the first time, the last atom of courage and fortitude is often severely disciplined until it becomes almost despair.

The sea may be as still as a mill pond in October. An ominous hush in the sluggish air holds fast to sleeping nature, when out of the yellowish sky, spring a spasmodic breeze, a quickly following wind, which roughen the distant horizon. As with a bound, from circling wind and wave tear forth the pent up hurricane. In a trice the peaceful scenes of nature are transformed into those of destruction and death. Junks are overturned and sunk like autumn leaves. Boom, boom goes a sea on our port, tearing through steel and iron, carrying Chinese sailors, servants, everything in its irresistible sway, and nearly swamping the vessel itself. Whack, whack, whack, crash, crash, crack, flush, amid howling of tempest and cry of man and beast, create, in fewer minutes than it takes to write, a sad and frightful pandemonium. A lull, a dark boiling flood, madly churning into foam, rolls stubbornly away and is soon lost to sight. Another lull, and swish-swash come spars, barrels, casks, boats, rigging and masts, up and around, as if in mute appeal for instant reinstatement. Chinese junks float helplessly on all sides, alike shorn of glory and bereft of their occupants. Also poor John Chinaman, "Alle samee Melican man!"

We soon found the sea a perfect type of Balboa's Pacific. Perfect quiet rested on its surface. A wavy undulation swept over the dark blue water and seemed to flow over the distant horizon like water in a basin. Now and then a large sea-fowl lay peacefully resting in the placid pool, and a large palm tree or remnant of wreckage mounted by gulls and looking like shipwrecked mortals floated aimlessly by. The busy mind soon caught the spell and, glad to rest, lay back in dreamy comfort.

The three days following were foggy, as the repeated fog-whistle constantly reminded us. Only a few whales appeared in the afternoon for diversion. The next day was Sunday, and besides the service, the

ROUTE IN THE EASTERN HEMISPHERE.

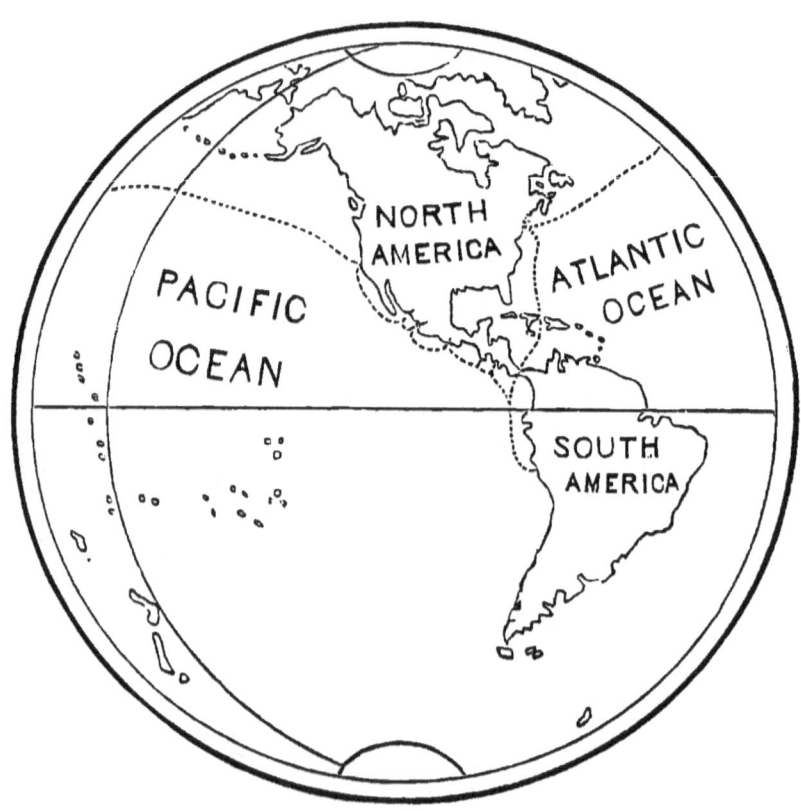

ROUTE IN THE WESTERN HEMISPHERE.

acquaintance of Ah You, a 16-year-old Chinese girl, who had been kidnapped, carried to San Francisco and sold for $1500, makes it worthy of mention. This was an attractive, well educated and refined Celestial, quite matter of fact, but pleasing and instructive withal. Her feet were large, however, quite as enormous as many of my gentle readers, but you must remember that the cruel custom of pinching and dwarfing the feet had begun to disappear at her birth, and now is wholly confined to those classes in society who, in custom as well as religion, live only in the past. So, my gentle reader, she had a well formed, plump little foot, with two rings on her big toes and two bands of silver on her shapely ankles. Her hair was as black as a raven, and large loops of gold and onyx graced her well-shaped ears. She was a good type of the higher and better class of that nation, as you will allow, when I tell you that she refused to be sold for gold and bravely sought our aid to escape even the appearance of sinning.

August 1 was also foggy, with a southwest wind, and, strange to say, as it was an unusual experience to me, a high sea running. The Atlantic was faithfully personated. The high peaks and deep valleys, the heavy thuds and overtopping waves, were piled up all about us, but a fog at the same time was unnatural anywhere.

The same experience was repeated on the following day, and still the more unusual one to me and most travellers, that of throwing away a whole day from the calendar. This we did on August 2, at four bells, noon. This was on account of our reaching the meridian of Greenwich in its extension around the globe. This change gave us two Sundays the same week, and put our log into east longitude, like the vessels we should have to meet farther on. My watch, which I carefully kept running Boston time, was several hours fast, — and reached 12 hours in the Malay Peninsula, indicating that I had travelled half my journey around the world.

The next day, the 4th, we were in a smooth sea again, and surrounded by countless nautili and jelly fish, with now and then the poisonous sun and devil-fish as companions, and here and there a whale and Arctic bird. This day would have been August 3 at any point east of the line, but on crossing the line we cast the 3d to the winds and called it the 4th, for the reasons stated.

August 5. More Arctic birds above and around, with indications of land or islands, which the officer said were of the Alaskan group. The sky was clouded. The next day was the same, with the bright exception that the sun gladdened our eyes in the afternoon. Careful observations, impossible for nearly a week, were then promptly taken, which made all breathe easier. Under the date of the following day I find in my diary: "By the loss of last Wednesday, Sunday comes a little unnaturally, but here it is again, and I have a hard time trying to make people understand that it is a fact. Bishop Warren held services as usual, but is far from well. The sea is fine and level, but the air is almost too warm for comfort. After my custom, read to officers and stewards." August 8 gave us a grand sea and better weather. The monsters of the deep sent up their arches and columns of spray in every direction. The two Japanese students seemed to take increased enjoyment as we neared their native land. One had taken a special degree at Oxford, England, and was now returning home to stay.

And this leads me to state that, wherever on this broad earth I have met this race, nothing but the pleasantest relations have sprung up between us. The happy hours have sped away only too quickly. From the general in the standing army to the humble servant in the hotel, the utmost courtesy and earnest interest have been manifested. No wonder, then, that the memory of the people as well as of their beautiful land, remains with all the freshness of yesterday. August 10, a frightful ground swell was accompanied by the strong equatorial current common here, and the first rain, except in tempest, we had seen since leaving San Francisco, 17 days before. Early the next morning, caught sight of Yokohama Light. Soon a cloud high in the sky parted and revealed a giant peak, well rounded and blue, with long white streaks of ice and snow running down to and hiding in the clouds below. Majestic crown! Mighty sentinel of a fairy land, Fusiyama!

CHAPTER V.

> O'er hill and mount,
> Through grove and dell,
> Lo, the land where fairies dwell!

THE first impressions of a place, like those of a person, are often worthier than the object. This does not hold true of Japan. Each day discloses something interesting, something new. Even the two recent outbreaks of old volcanoes are in point, although the third, destroying five villages in the Bandai region, is truly sad. No land boasts of grander mountain king than Fusian or Fusiyama. Closely following the uplifting mist, which brought us face to face with that gigantic form looking down from sparkling diadems of ice in quiet grandeur on our pigmy vessel, rose steep hills with deep ravines in full garb of velvet green.

After obtaining a clear view, I found the surface of the water covered with fishing junks, some with straw matting sails, others being sculled along with an ungainly long pole with a paddle tied to its water end, and worked from the vessel's side. Many of these queer craft seemed occupied by whole families as naked and black as Hottentots. The first to bear down upon us, with its prow deep in the water and stern high in the air, ludicrously reminded us of our good old great-grandmother's days and her high-heeled slipper, for we have nothing but this in America to furnish a fair comparison. Another striking feature is that no iron is used in their construction, for they are neatly dovetailed and joined, and often smoothed down to a fine finish, so that they might be said to have been Japanned. Just imagine such a queer craft, with stark naked bronze figures, with hair sticking straight up into the air, silently but surely closing in upon you from all directions, and on nearer approach seen to grasp long pikes with grappling iron or wooden hook, as if they meant business! I afterwards became accustomed to it, as I found, if one will travel in the Pacific and Indian Oceans, he must accept it as a necessary evil or custom, call it what you will.

After passing two small coast settlements we saw the rising ground on the left of Yokohama, and soon reached the harbor. It is a pretty piece of water as you enter. The European and American when they can, except the U. S. Consulate, have located, and established hospitals on the high ground before mentioned. The low ground is unhealthy in summer on account of the sewage in its canals. The year before my visit, nearly 100 people had been carried off by cholera daily. Many foreigners left for China and the United States to escape danger. Next to these hospitals, but further to the North, is another high elevation. renowned for its military and religious history, that contains some queer old slab-like monuments stuck deep in the ground, like so many huge grave-stones. This was the first spot I visited, as it seemed to give me the best view of Yokohama, the long winding river to Tokio and the surroundings. There I ate my first Japanese lunch, and partook of their sweetmeats and excellent tea. The tiny cups, so fragile as to be easily crushed between thumb and forefinger, were served by two bright but timid maidens that were lovely enough for Cinderellas.

But, as I have heretofore done, I am anticipating. While forging up the harbor against the strong current, on turning my glass to the rear, I perceived that we were closely followed by a Canadian Pacific steamer, the very one, probably, that would have conveyed me hither, had I decided to take the American overland journey of that new line. Just before us lay their *Batavia*, once plying between New York and Liverpool on the Cunard line, crippled by being caught in the recent typhoon. Now out of style, and rusty, she seemed almost patriarchal. Passing one native steamer, and another from China, we crowded on all speed, and curved around to where a United States man-of-war rode at anchor, and with a boom from our gun, quickly cast our anchors.

Before our motion ceased, rap-tat-tap, some hundred of bamboo poles fasten to the rail, and crew and officers quickly become engaged in a hand-to-hand struggle to keep the natives from boarding the vessel. In spite of the danger, it was a most amusing scene,—men, women and children recklessly sculled on their slight but ungainly sampans, thrusting the weaker aside, and, too eager to get a fare, to notice the conflict on gangway and side, calling out till their stiff, porcupine, black hair seemed to dart out little javelins. The hot sun of mid-day smote upon their wet, bare limbs and heads like the flash of a sword. The babies awakened, caught up the cry, and pandemonium reigned. After a score or more got seriously hurt, the rest become more governable. They took to their sampans like monkeys from a hot potato, greedily eyeing the gangway, and springing out at the first passenger so unlucky as to be obliged to go ashore.

With a Japanese friend, I stood under shelter, and saw a lone Chinaman carefully pick up his treasure, all contained in one small bundle, and carefully pick his way down the steps. We were then riding some twelve feet high. Up sprang a forest of hooked poles, in fear that some more fortunate Jap might get the prize. Each of the hooks went straight for venturesome John, and held fast to bundle, trousers, man and queue itself. All now began quietly pulling in different directions. As the resultant force of all this motive power was downward, of course downward poor John had to go. There was a terribly disfiguring look on his usually stolid countenance, something like that of a cat drawn by the tail. It was shameful, and everything was done to prevent and stop such an outrage. Down he had to go, nevertheless, while blows were showered on the heads of the perpetrators with as little effect as an iron crowbar on that of an active but misguided bulldog. When he reached the lowest step, five or more sampans awaited his coming, and twice that number of eager boatsmen soon had strong hold of his outposts.

Then came the tug of war. Amid bawling and fighting, pushing this sampan out, and that one in, the whole lot were precipitated into the briny deep, and poor John, with little clothing and less hair, was at last dragged, half choked, into the nearest boat. Then came a fight for his baggage. One tantalizingly holds out the bundle from the water, and a second tries to allure the almost breathless owner over the rest into his craft, while another with remnants of queue and clothing, pursues a like course in another direction. John is a study. Hundreds of throats from the vessel's side seem to burst out at once like so many cannon, and hundreds of decayed oranges, pine apples, eggs and turnips fly into the soon gaping crowd like magic. The bundle is snatched by a hook. The man, refusing to release his hold, is suddenly jerked, bundle and all, into the sea. After a few well-directed blows, he changed his mind, and was glad to be helped into his boat again, empty-handed.

Strange to say, although this serves to illustrate a

common experience, the participants seem to take any result in good part, as a mere matter of business. I need not add, also, that none but a Jap or Chinaman would be treated in this harsh way, although here, as at Alexandria, you are annoyed beyond patience by pulling and pushing. I need not say, either, that my conveyance to the shore was by sampan, and that, too, with the two ungainly fifteen-foot sculls, worked by two bright little boys less than 10 years of age, and that I had a most pleasant and attractive journey.

A long strip of land, with side paved to the water, and extending into the bay at the foot of the Custom House, and literally covered by sampans, is where we were first set on shore. No sooner had we gained our feet, and paid our fare of 20 sen, than there came rushing down upon us a score or more of little covered gigs, not much larger or stronger than a good-sized baby carriage. Each was drawn by a short but trim-looking man, who quickly halted at my side and pleasantly inquired, "Rickisha? rickisha?" My companion and I, each, stepped into one, and side by side, we bowled along the smooth streets to a money-broker's office for exchange. I was not surprised to find the broker a Chinaman, although I confess to a little disappointment. His treatment, however, was fair and courteous. He gave me $6.50 in yens, sens and smaller coins, for every $5 in gold I would transfer to his itching palm. At Colon, we had been offered $16 for a

$10 gold piece, both countries paying us silver, but my practice was to take only the amount really needed for expenses, as it saved me the annoyance of carrying it about. The tempo, represented at the end of the last chapter but one, is fast getting rare, and, really, is an awkward coin to handle. It is elliptical, of copper, and has the customary square hole in its centre for the purpose of stringing it on the iron or wire upright commonly seen in the shops of both Japan and China. This, with the reckoning machine, meets you everywhere. If you buy but a sash, out comes the machine, and the merchant's fingers run deftly over his little wooden disks until the sum is found, and, on payment, your coin is quickly strung to complete the purchase.

The new silver coinage, of the yen, the sen and its sub-divisions are, however, fashioned solid, like our coin, and are very attractive to the common people. They contain an inscription of the National dragon on one side, and a wreath on the other. Paper money. in little strips, is also in use, reminding us of our shinplaster days of the war. They have a neat and commodious railroad station, convenient to merchant and trader. The level tract on which most of the business-houses stand is right at the water's edge, convenient. but not so desirable in point of health. Religiously and educationally, the United States and New England are well represented here, as their places of business abundantly show, and had we been content to leave Japan with no knowledge of the inland cities and towns, we would have departed, I think, with a sense of pleasure that only comes from appreciation of a worthy object

One fine morning, we were drawn to the station by our jinrickisha men for a trip to the capital, now called Tokio. Scores of these little busy vehicles were going the same way. Old men, on foot with pretty little children out for a walk, seemed everywhere, while many a mother, with her little one clinging pig-aback, hurried along to work or to market. All wore wooden clogs or sandals, raised high from the ground, with a strap often between the index toe, if I may so speak, and its next neighbor, necessitating the curiosity of a mitten-shaped stocking. In the muddiest weather you see neat white socks perching on these high wooden stilts, so to speak, and if one slip off and you spy the aperture before mentioned, do not shrink back as if it were a rent, for it is all for a useful purpose. Surely it is not additional proof of the Darwin theory. Alighting at the station, a mother passed on before me. Down from her back slips a tiny child. Tap-tap go two little clogs on the pavement, and straight as an arrow, without use of form or hands, two little mittened feet slip like mice into their shallow recesses, and like a quail chicken with shell on back, away trips the little chap after his fast retreating dame.

Tokio is about 18 miles north of Yokohama and can

be reached, by water or by rail, in about an hour's ride. While waiting, in comes a woman of 50, accompanied by a maiden of about 16 years. Neither has hat or head covering, but rich folds of jet black tresses, carefully arranged in broad plaits, alone are seen. The younger is lovely in shape and personal attractions, but a bright bare spot glares out from the crown of her otherwise fair head, a pink flesh spot that you want to clap a plaster upon, and say, "For Heaven's sake, my dear, do go and dress yourself!" The elder smiled upon her comrade with effusion, and in that smile — horrors! her teeth were in deep mourning. I had forgotten that they here require, in the married women, two rows of black, mummy-like ivories, from fear of a kiss. No one could imagine doing it; why not then let the pearls grow, they would drop out soon enough. I had no sooner recovered from my disgust, when in marched some sixty men with long wooden pikes, ten feet in length or more. Shield-like hats, made of palm or straw, rested on one arm, and coarse mantles of like material upon their shoulders, while coarse grass sandals appeared strapped to their feet. Examining them closely, I concluded they were not soldiers, as they had no weapons except the long smooth stock or pike. An official soon came forward and deprived them of these, and, to my inquiries, stated they were people from the interior going up to Tokio on a holiday. I somehow felt that I had lost a victory. Yet they were a more martial and formidable body than the white-gloved garrison I afterward found at the capital.

At last the short train, with its tiny cars, bore us from the station, by thatched hovel, groups of round-topped houses, queer image-like graveyard stones, and out into the wide rice fields and richly cultivated country. Large water lilies, three feet high and bearing a flower as large as the Victoria regia, thickly lined the meadows. Apple and persimmon trees, laden with rich fruit, clung to low wooden supports, and beans, radishes, onions and tea seemed everywhere. The rice fields are divided by ridges of land, so that, after the one-handled plough has been drawn through, by coolies or an ox, and the rice shoots are fully set, water may be turned on to keep the soil in proper condition for rapid growth. After the rice is cut with their straight-bladed and long-handled sickles, and the straw laid aside for thatch, wheat is sown. Three crops are raised on the same spot yearly, thus keeping agricultural Japan like a garden. Four crops of alfalfa were shown me in California, raised in one year from the same land; but the rotation of crops, as practised in Japan, is far better for the land. The apple referred to is of fine russet color, has the flavor and internal appearance of a pear, and **is raised** by training the tree to an arbor. It is almost tasteless, however. On the other hand, the persimmon is rich, sweet and juicy.

But on we sped, passing a factory or two, and a machine shop under French engineers, till the old forts barring the river, four in number, round and glistening like polished marble, suddenly flashed into view. Yet on, to the old castle and palace of the Mikado, where Gen. Grant was received a few years ago, and we find ourselves within the commodious station at Tokio. The place is located on a plain, with some attractive heights here and there adjoining and relieving it. When it was of less importance, it was known as Yeddo. It now is a city of a million and a half inhabitants, and extends nine miles in length and five miles in breadth. Its old temples are the best preserved in all Japan,—Iyiyasu, one, if not their greatest hero, having given it large patronage,—Iyiyasu, who raised Yeddo from obscurity to the leading city and stronghold of all Japan, and whose remains, removed from the whispering cedar and booming sea at Kuno-Kan, now rest among the shady groves and bright lakes of Nik-ko. There Buddha was first introduced by a Shinto deity. High on the mountain side rises a grand mausolum, the present resting place of all that is mortal of this the greatest Mikado, "The Great Light of the East, the Great Incarnation of Buddha."

Until the latter part of the sixth century, Shintoism was the prevailing religion, but it was little better than a political creed. Nichiron, I am told, although a Shintoist, early began to teach that if Buddha be obeyed and followed, man would become a part of him in the great hereafter; if not, man will suffer repeated deaths and final annihilation. All are supposed to have had a prior existence, and to be destined to suffer again after death here, and go on from one life to another until the soul attains its highest purity. This is the same religion that you find from Egypt to Japan, with Hindoo, Malay, Chinese and Japanese, comprising more devotees than any other religion on the face of the globe; but, despite all its temples, groves and forms, there is no outward observance, except on holidays, and little vital religion here, as elsewhere, unless it be politeness. Sea, land, and sky combine to make the land beautiful and sublime, and the belief in a former existence and future probation is a fitting accompaniment.

As we stepped from the station to the pavement, long lines of the ubiquitous rickisha moved down upon us, so much like child's play as to create a laugh, but in we step, and are, by direction, driven to the Consulate, and then, with the necessary permit, around to the old palace, closely walled to the very water's edge. Then off again, over bridge, down street, through the liliputian bazaars, which are inimitable, except by children in their play.

There are but a very few houses in either Japan or China above two stories, — hotels, warehouses, and palaces being an exception. Most of them are low

JAPANESE TEMPLE AT NIKKO.

studded, and remind you of seaside cottages at home, except the whole front is open, and, if closed at all, closed by lattice work or paper slides, the paper serving instead of glass, to admit the light. The floor is always raised a foot or more, and, as you walk or ride by, you get a full view of their household economy. The floors are divided into rooms by this same sliding screen of paper or, among the wealthier class, of silk and ornamental frames.

Upon a dais, set like a picture in its frame, a Japanese maiden, with clasped hands and bright face turned upward to the rising sun, may sometimes be seen at her morning devotion. The very next neighbor may be an artisan, busily at work in a corresponding room. Such is life, the dwelling usually serving, even in its best room, for a workshop, art gallery, — and then they are always curious and attractive, — and reception-room. It would require a volume to describe the variety of lacquer ware, carved ivory, embroidered silk, and hand-painted screens, pottery and bronze, which you find everywhere in full view on the leading streets. As in its forests, you see the tiniest moss and fern by the side of the noblest pine, so in Tokio, you find from the frailest cup to the eternal bronze.

Even if I go on, how can I give an adequate idea of Tokio! Its temples, its old castle, reached by almost countless stone steps at an angle of 80 deg. or more, its University and scientific schools, its white-gloved and white-robed military, standing at little boxes on the street corners, its volcanic mountains and earthquake river valleys, its scarcity of bird and insect, its rare abundance of fish and flower, pen fails to represent. For the temples, it is enough to say that, although quaint, grotesque and elaborate, they are, at the same time, gaudy and cheap, and their shrines and priests a relic of barbarism. Yet I removed my shoes and tramped them over, out of respect for the persevering and enthusiastic toilers that spent a life, perhaps, in their perfection. The dragon, the stork, and the large mouthed and terror-inspiring deity, crop out everywhere. So does the American as a tourist, for in exchange for the yen I handed the priest, the temple's coffers yielded up an Italian lira and a United States nickel five-cent piece, which were handed me with a smile by the plump little fellow who knew I was American.

There was an eclipse of the sun that day, and astronomers from all parts of the world had met for observations, and in the absent-mindedness peculiar to home clergymen and scientists, the nickel was probably passed off for a fifty-cent admission. Although the sky is laden with dew and rain, and keeps the rich soil capable of yielding sixty-fold of rice, tea, millet and cotton, it smiled my whole stay, like the bright-eyed maidens beneath it. The present Mikado is but 36 years old, and, unlike the ruler of old kept concealed by shogun and daimio, he seeks the best and most progressive in Germany, France, England and the United States, and now promises to his people in 1890 as free a country as Old England. Long live both ruler and people, to whom it is nature itself to be graceful, courteous and happy!

It was with sinking heart that I bid adieu. It is with feelings of homesicknesss that I now revive the memory. The last I saw of its interesting shores, after Fusi-an, with its ice-bound summit, were its two active volcanoes, Smoking Jack, and another the name of which has gone from memory. The inland sea, with mirror-like surface and green slopes, — even Nagasaki, about the size of Yokohama, but dealing in coal instead of indigo, rice, tea and silk, as in the latter place, soon passed out of view, and nothing but the calm, blue sea, with its flashing flying fish remained to sustain our sinking spirits. Countries, like individuals, attract and repel, and nothing could have been more deplorable to one in our over-strained condition, than the change from Japan to China.

Shanghai and Amoy we will not describe. Formosa we saw next, but its wildness, both of people and shores, hardly deserves our time, though for the first time we met with the little rectangular bar of silver, worth about $1.50 in our money, in use as coin, and an animal resembling our prairie bison, used for motive power, both of which were of some interest. A good part of the coast of China, down to the Pearl river, is hilly, with now and then a deep ravine or low plain. The rivers appear in places to have repeatedly changed their course, and the hills appear barren, compared with Japan. Acres of whales' food, palm trees and Chinese fishing junks swarmed around our boat, until it seemed as though we must stop, or run the latter down. But in those quiet days, tilted back under the deck's awning, we loved to recline, drinking in the fresh breeze and talking of Ward and Chinese Gordon, the foreign Chinese heroes, of whom the latter had lately met so brave and heroic a death in the Soudan, and who had not long before sailed our very course.

They were dreamy days, and not altogether unprofitable. But one day, while thus employed, a friend came running up and, in his inability to speak English, caught hold of my arm and led me forward down the companion-way. He excitedly pointed to some fifty or more Chinamen grouped around the vessel's side. They seemed so serious and businesslike I, at first, failed to see the cause for my companion's excitement, but, on approaching nearer, the first thing that caught my eye was a long-necked goose, stuffed and cooked nice and brown, its mouth full of bon-bons, and the rest bedecked with celery, joss sticks and what not, in close communion with a plump, crisp and juicy pig fit for a king. A quick upward movement of those grim-visaged Celestials sent goose, pig and all far over the vessel's side, and followed them with handfuls of strips of paper called prayers. It was a strange and, to me, amusing scene, but the decorum was that of a funeral. It seems that a steamer, called the "Japan," with several hundreds of Chinese, had some years before gone down at this point, and that all true Chinese were expected to offer prayers and sacrifice to the Jost of the sea in their behalf.

Far in the distance we saw the heights of Southern China, a long line of smoke indicating the presence of a sister boat in advance. By a little starboard movement, we were able to see a narrow, zigzag passage between high, abrupt hills, into which we soon hastened. How a sailing vessel can enter is a mystery, yet here they are, until the channel becomes too narrow for other than our own, when down shoots the sun pitilessly upon our heads. We can feel it, like a knife, through the thick canvas awnings. On the left, Chinese are toiling up the steep banks in the construction of a new fortification. On the right, large oval white spots appear upon the hillsides. By my glass, they closely resemble marble disks. A medical friend, who had a little knowledge of the place, informed me that they were Chinese tombs. These I found elsewhere, especially at Canton, where whole hills were devoted to the same cave-like burials. But on we forge, the high mountains on the left, the hills on our right, till we catch sight of a signal station, followed by a long line of buildings unmistakably European or American, we could not tell which. With increased speed, we stand to port, and a neat oval harbor, nearly land-locked, with vessels of all nations, suddenly comes into view. A little beyond, to the left, rose high mountains, precipitous and rocky, with a very small plain covered with modern houses down to the very water's edge, while others seemed climbing and hanging to craggs where iron rivet and chain, alone, held back impending ruin.

This was Hong Kong, the principal port for the Chinese silk and tea trade. On we glide till, with a graceful curve and booming guns, we announce our arrival and let slip the anchor chains. Who would imagine a settlement in this queer, isolated spot! It seemed like finding the cave of Capt. Kidd in the Bahamas. Taking a Chinese sail-boat, we went ashore. The husband and son manned the sails, the wife and daughters steered our course, while one or two of their almond-eyed little ones crawled up from behind, fell upon our necks, and peaked curiously around into our faces. Such mites of humanity, such attentive and insinuating little rascals, we forgot our shirt bosoms and let them hug. But it was a genuine water home for the whole family. Summer and winter finds this numerous family hived within its narrow walls. But what more shall we say of this people, so characteristically opposite to us in daily life and custom.

Some one has said, "This is a country where the

roses have no fragrance and the women no petticoats; where the laborer has no Sabbath, the magistrate no sense of honor; where the needle points to the South, and the sign of being puzzled is to scratch the antipodes of the head; where the place of honor is on the left hand, and the seat of intellect is in the stomach; where to take off your hat is an insolent gesture, and to wear white garments is to put yourself into mourning." Speaking of dress, its outward appearance is the same both for male and female, with the exception that the frock and trousers of the latter are broader and more flowing. If you look for style, your disappointment will be great and lasting. And yet Hong Kong is not the best place in which to study the Chinese, as they are too much under English influence to appear fully natural. In some parts of China, although shape or style remains the same, there is a great affectation of delicate color and ornamentation.

Should any one desire to appear a la Chinese, just snatch up, immediately on rising, your two pillow-cases, and never so negligently join them at the open ends. Clip off the ends opposite, and boldly don them. You are half Chinese, my friend. Hurriedly cut in your bolster covering, if you have one, two good-sized slits towards one end, for the arms, and make another aperture large enough for the insertion of the head. Taking it for granted that you have put the first articles on your lower extremities, you have but to carelessly throw the last over your head, insert your arms, and perhaps pull the article down a trifle, and you are in full costume. You feel queer, and conscious, perhaps, that you look still more so. Your ankles refused to be covered, and the arm bashfully draws up its full length. It makes your appearance none the less true. You are in mourning, too. That, no doubt, will end the experiment. Many a time have I seen these Celestials in those pillow-cases, and the only additional article of dress a towel, slit in the middle for the neck, hanging down fore-and-aft, so to speak, and caught together with cloth loops and buttons.

When we first came to anchor, the usual active and boisterous scenes of Japanese and Chinese ports were again enacted. Long, bamboo hooked-poles were, in the twinkling of an eye, fastened to the rail, and four, five, sometimes more, natives clambered, like so many rats, up their dizzy and dangerous heights on the same pole to deck. As I was looking on, one snapped, and down crashed the whole string of struggling humanity upon the boats below. It would have killed anything but a Chinaman. I could not see even a change of countenance among the entire number. The same stolid look, up-and-try-it-again expression, accompanied them to a renewed attempt. I need not detail again such a scene. The one at Yokohama, although mild in comparison, is a good illustration of greed for passengers in these isolated countries. Steamers as large as ours have been attacked in open sea, boarded and overrun by swarms of these Chinese rats, before anything but hot water could be turned upon them. They call them pirates there, and even since my return, the San Pablo has fallen a victim to their rapacity by burning.

On my pleasant sail with the family referred to, inspection of boat life was easy. Everything was scrupulously clean. The boat was a sampan, with two wide awnings for shelter from the rain and sun, one amidships, and the other over the stern, where the wife, daughters and babies were located. It was here, also, that I was placed. There was a good breeze, and the Chinese sail is peculiarly adapted for well-regulated power. It is similar to a bat's wing. Radiating spars extend across its whole surface, which can be reefed like a fan, and almost as easily, so that, while danger is averted, speed is regulated, and you fairly glide along, skimming the water like a bird. When landed, two coolies strung my baggage on a bamboo and ran away, like deer, to the hotel. Hong Kong has two of the finest hotels in the whole world. The same may be said of several of its places of business, but it is so closed in from the sea that many Europeans have sought the heights, thousands of feet above, to get a breath of air. Punkas, or long hangings fastened on the upper edge to the ceiling, are kept in motion by coolies pulling an attached cord. Its fan-like motion sends a constant current of cooling air in both directions. The heat would often be unbearable otherwise. This simple invention is in use from Japan to the Mediterranean. In the saloon of ocean steamers it is stationed directly above the tables, and is generally kept in motion only at meal time, when its grateful fanning is as dear to the traveller as a zephyr in the desert.

As I write, my evening paper relates that cholera is fast decimating the European settlements at Hong Kong. That dreaded disease, as well as small-pox, is always to be met, summer or winter, in this land of flowers and heathen. The Emperor, in 1875, fell a victim to the latter, and many a poor fellow who left home a bright, rosy Scotch or English lad, told me how his heart ached to return to his aged parents and family, because his disfigurement by that awful curse seemed too great a humiliation for him to force upon their loving eyes. Whenever I met such a one, he clung to me, although a stranger, in such speechless pathos, it often became painful.

By day, the streets of Hong Kong are nearly impassable on account of the number of jinrickishas, sedan chairs and coolies, and, to my surprise, the European does not hesitate to curse, strike, and even knock down the Chinaman who is so unlucky as to get in his way. A few miles across the harbor and you might see the tables turned. John will put up with anything if he can only earn money, and he knows that he must stand the cuffs of the European if he wants his coppers; so he grins and bears it. He cannot be out on the streets at night later than 8 o'clock, and has to do his gambling and opium smoking in secret. Fifteen thousand in three years are said to have left here for the United States. There are some 15 consuls of different nations, and about ten banking-houses here, but, as it is a free port and really belongs to England, I do not know the amount of trade. It is immense, however. Kohloon, right across the harbor, is another breathing-place for resident Europeans.

But let us take a side-wheel steamer for Canton, which lies some 75 miles northwest of Victoria or Hong Kong, as it is called. The boat draws but little water, and so lies at the wharf a little south of the hotel. She easily swings off and slowly steams down to the mouth of the Pearl River, on which Canton with its canal and narrow winding house-rafts is located. Our companions are all Chinamen. We think of rats and lice. You really thank heaven that the Mandarins of this benighted land have set their condemnation on railroads. It is a lucky escape from the three-in-a-seat system you feel would here prevail. Do you see that dark-skinned, monkey-faced John squat on the deck? Yes. You notice that he has removed his only upper garment, a flimsy, dilapidated affair, and, having turned it inside out, seems strangely contemplative. If you will step nearer you will observe a smile play over his usually taciturn features as he swoops down upon a little spot of activity within the folds of said raiment. With a deftness, gained only by long practice, there is a sudden transfer of hand to mouth, and, although fully convinced that the wicked flea no man pursueth, you quickly beat a retreat. With hill on each side, for eight hours you pursue the even tenor of your way, till a high pagoda, thickly massed sampans, rafts containing whole families, and large warehouses come suddenly into view. The banks are lined with sampans, and the shore and streets swarm with the pigmy Chinamen, while above, with the exception of several pagodas and temples piercing the air, there is nothing but a plain of red-tiled roofs.

Canton is well walled, however, and, it would seem, regularly laid out, but none of the streets are more than eight or ten feet in width, and, in your chair, carried by being swung from the shoulders of from two to four coolies, you are in mortal fear of causing serious damage to shins, if no other property, of busy John. Mahometanism as well as Buddhism is represented by an ancient temple. The English and French for years have at times controlled the destiny of the place, and many a siege it has been obliged to undergo before reaching its present state. Whole hills, on one side, are devoted to graves and tombs for the dead. One of the largest temples, a Buddhist, called the "Temple of the Ocean Banner," covers seven acres of ground, is surrounded by a wall and laid out into courts. Here also are gardens and a cemetery for the ashes of the priests, whose bodies are usually burned. There are about 2,000 nuns and priests in the city, nearly all of whom belong to Buddhist temples. These are gloomy, uninteresting structures. One visit suffices. Even where the idol sits or lies enshrined, there is but feeble light, and that only in front. The Mosque is an angular, tapering tower, about 160 feet high, erected by Arabian adventurers centuries ago. A pagoda of nine stories, octagonal in form and 170 feet high, thirteen centuries old, stands near the west gate.

The market in Japan contained shark and other strange food, but here it was a source of still greater amusement. My readers may not know that the Chinese use no milk nor any of its products, as cheese or butter. Among their delicacies we observed, as in a dream, cats, dogs—not in the form of sausage, but plain matter-of-fact dog-meat—owls, hawks, horse-flesh, rodents, and edible birds' nests. Surely, if these are delicacies, it is not hard to understand how industrious John lives and thrives where others would starve. There are many other curious things in this immense country that really have an abiding interest. There is the tallow tree; there is the wax insect which, placed on the leaves of a tree, after a short time leaves a waxy deposit, which is removed and thrown into boilers and rendered into solid wax, and afterward moulded into sugar-loaf cakes. There is the camphor laurel, the blacking tree, the bamboo, the lichee, bearing a pleasant fruit in grape-like clusters, each enclosed in a covering similar to the oak ball; the varnish tree; the mulberry, upon which millions of silkworms, on fan-like palms, are ravenously and noisily feeding. Even silk is found wild. There are rubies, precious stones, fire-crackers and palm-leaf fans, which are exported to New York alone to the amount of $5,000,000 annually, cassia buds, and about Amoy, the well-known Bohea tea, which is erroneously called after the Woo-e Mountains in its neighborhood. Amoy also exports sugar and fine sugar candies, but the Island of Formosa, opposite, is still richer .in sugar, and also exports largely sulphur, jute, camphor, grass cloth and rice paper. In places the rivers, in summer, carry down to the plains their burden of sediment and leave it bare on their banks. The following winter finds the industrious Celestial busily washing from its varied constituents the bright yellow gold. Hemp grows often more than 12 feet in height for miles.

Thus might one go on about this busy yet stagnant land, the rich Cathay of the Middle Ages. In 1247, some one writes of this strange land: "The country is very rich in corn, in wine, in gold and silver, in silk, and every kind of produce for the support of mankind. The sea lies between it and India. These

Cathayans are little fellows, speaking much through the nose, and have very narrow eyes. The common money consists of pieces of cotton paper, about a palm in length and breadth, upon which certain lines are printed. They do their writing with a pencil, such as painters paint with, and a single character of theirs comprehends several letters, so as to form a whole word." It is hoped that their cotton money never served them the rascally turn of our linen paper money in 1862. It is interesting to note its existence at that early date, as well as the use of the brush instead of the pen in writing, just as they do to-day. They manipulate it with all the skill of an artist, and, as almost every one can read and write, the eye is early trained and passable artists made of all. Here printing was invented eight centuries or more in advance of Guttenburg, and here Columbus bent his adventurous eye when he sailed west from Cadiz. Then Cathay and Zipangun; or China and Japan, were the El Dorado of all Europe. Nothing could exceed the fabulous riches they were reported to contain. But age and precedent are not marked by inventions alone. Moral training and social influence run in the same old beaten track, and among a good deal that seems strange and undesirable something might be learned with profit by the people of our own country.

One thing is filial piety, the respect and love of parent for child and child for parent, whatever be the age, condition, or estate. You see miles of boats and rafts on the rivers, apparently overrun with people, who live thereon the year round. You see their small, one, or at best, two-storied dwellings, similarly crowded with humanity. Why? Do not set it down to economy alone, for it is largely from filial affection. As soon as a son is able to take care of himself, he does not run away from home, or ungratefully curse his parent for no better support or condition, but puts his shoulder to the wheel and makes it move more easily.

Then too a wife is early sought, by some female go-between, and, if acceptable, the son presents her with a little book bearing the impress of a dragon on one side and a phœnix on the other, emblems of conjugal fidelity. If both families are satisfied, she is brought home, thus forming around the old a nucleus for a new household. This seems a redeeming feature to many of their dark ways. Frugal, persevering, enlightened, they are the equal of any race, but without these qualities they, as any other like people, are a curse to the neighborhood they infest. The compression of the feet of their female infants is a practice slowly decaying, yet, on all sides, that naked member still thrusts its tortured shape before your critical eye. The width of the foot often seems unnatural, and beneath the arch, so beautiful in the natural member, runs an ugly depression, while above the prominent heel is another fissure still more deforming. Surely, a whole field of corns is of rarer loveliness than this monstrosity. But it is intended for a covering of sock and slipper! A good illustration of modern morality!

A CHINESE NUT.

CHAPTER VI.

*In India's spicy breezes bathed,
Peace to mind and heart.*

ON my return to Hong Kong, I remained barely long enough to dine with a friend at his neighboring bungalow, and inspect the Indian Sepoy, the Sikh guards and soldiers of the English garrison, now renowned for their physical and manly beauty. By midday we were aboard an East India steamer, and at once under full speed, were ploughing along to the

China Sea. Without looking after baggage, I climbed to the bridge, but found myself confronted by an active and apparently earnest bull-dog, which eyed me with an expression that plainly meant business. As he seemed to have no human companions, and I no animal friends, my only safety was to boldly push on. And on I went, despite the quickly curling lip and formidable array of glistening teeth. I remember calling — gently, I thought — the horrid beast, "Beauty," but why, except from a forced conviction that the way he could take hold was most pointedly expressed by that term, passes all comprehension. It cannot be from love. My memory will not allow me to say it was from sarcasm. With a swing to the left, I landed in the lower wheel-house, where I snatched up a handy marine glass and shot out its long sections square into the bounding brute's eyes.

With a loud, short bark, he crouched upon his stumpy legs and sprang to this side, then that, in joyous play, as if to say, "How glad I am to see you. I have been dozing in the sun, and my eyes at first took you for a heathen. You have come to play, I see. Let me just have hold of that end?" That end, he had often had hold of, a fact clearly proven by the many little dents and scratches along its otherwise smooth surface. Fully recognizing the value of caution, when dealing with the grinning, either dog or man, I suffered not the wily foe to get around to the rear, but kept him amused until I had gained the upper bridge, with which Eastern vessels are now supplied. There I found the Captain, chief officer, and a Malay quartermaster. The wheel of this upper bridge did not exceed a foot in diameter, and could be controlled with two fingers, the steering power really being done by steam. The quickness and reliability, as well as ease, of guiding such a mighty object as the ocean steamship amid the many little islands and channels found here, and often so suddenly approached that even the united force of four men, as are often needed at the wheel of some vessels, strike one as marvellous.

A loud cry from the deck caused me to step to the rail and look down. Hundreds of Chinese stood before me wildly gesticulating and pointing to their native shore. A boat on our port was being towed along at a speed which almost lifted it bodily out of the water, and I had about concluded the outcry to be nothing more than a signal to throw off the tow-line, when a stalwart John came rushing down the deck and began belaboring all about him with a stout cane. Splash — thud — splash again, and then so often, we turned to the water. One Chinaman had sprung over the rail, directly in front of the racing junk, and had been struck with force enough to kill. Up he rose, however, and struck boldly out for the neighboring shore. Another followed, then another and another, till a score or more were earnestly making for liberty.

On, faster and faster, we cleft the quiet water, till some one succeeded at last in casting off the tow and thus securing quiet.

As I looked down on the unhappy faces below, I recalled a statement made to us before starting, that we were to carry out to the East Indies, on contracts of one or more years, several hundreds of Chinese as plantation laborers. These had never left their homes or native land before, and had been tempted to come aboard and undertake the journey on the promise of 50 or so silver dollars a year. It is little better than slavery, and as soon as their native shores began to recede, thoughts of home proved too strong for the coveted bribe, so pell-mell over they plunged, like porpoises in a breeze, too much excited to realize danger either from boat or sea. It was a strange sight, and meant escape from harsh treatment, poor food and cruel blows, a worse fate than that of our slave in 1860, so we looked on in speechless sympathy. There were sullen brows that night, and many a day thereafter, as little knots of dark-visaged coolies crowded together and discussed the situation. But we were in the teeth of a stiff S. W. monsoon, that piled the deck high with foaming billows that drove the unfortunate cooley below.

The Chinese Sea can be strong and beautiful, but never gentle and quiet before a monsoon. Up, up, rose our gallant ship, and then like a dolphin, straight as an arrow, down plunged her nose into the very depths. For several days we experienced just such wild and dangerous treatment. The coast of Anam rose high to the starboard, until we passed Hue and came to Saigon, the scene of the French war with the Black Flags, when it gradually became more low and sandy. I was told that the elephant, tiger and panther still run wild along these shores, but we were not so fortunate as to meet any, though we saw fires at night built for protection from them. Bankok, the capital of Siam, lies around to the right, but quite 30 miles up the river. Our steamer was too large to get across the bar. and, to my regret, I was obliged to forego my visit to the Sacred Elephants. My zeal was somewhat compensated by looking at the surrounding country, and in meeting a young Scotchman just returned from that city, who related his experience, but one much too long for insertion here. His story was, that there are two barns or places for the sacred white elephants of the Emperor, and that one was open to all. He also repeated the story—which occurred to me as old—that one day the Empress was being conveyed across the water, and as all on board were faithful subjects and had been taught that death would be meted out to him who should be so sacrilegious as to lay his hand on Her Majesty, they kept piously aloof, and when by accident she happened to slip into the treacherous deep, they stood quite as piously looking on, and let her drown.

I believe it is merely another version of Johnny Sands. "And she went in, of course. I can't, my dear, though much I wish, but you have tied my hands."

But what shall we say of one of the largest islands of the whole world, which I soon found right in my path, and which also presents the queer status of a rapidly-growing, or rising island. Borneo is but little known, except on its coast, and a few miles towards the interior, but Sarawak lies in so temperate a climate, and not so far from the equator, we may say a few words of this part of the strange land. The Dutch seem to control a good part of the island, though the English, since the advent of Sir James Brooke in 1846, have taken no slight part in the commerce and mining. Besides coal, antimony, copper, iron, tin, gold, diamonds, quicksilver, platina, sulphur, marble, and even petroleum, are found in paying quantities. There seem to be no active volcanoes about, although its peaks are certainly those of old activity, and that reminds me that while looking upon the old crater of Fusiyama, with its fires supplanted by perennial ice and snow, we could not help believing that it might once again burst out in all its old-time power and grandeur, and my evening's paper recounts an outbreak of a companion with the loss of 300 lives and 1,000 injured. True, that is Japan, but, as the earthquake and coral insect is constantly adding to Borneo's immense domain, it will not be strange that the eathquake may sometime give way to the mountain outbreak. The elephant, rhinoceros, ourang-outang and many forms of ape, the honey bear, oxen, pigs, crocodile, deer, boa-constrictor and eagle, run wild. Among the palms, the cocoanut and sago are the most important. Slavery still exists in the island. Kuching is the principal place, and a nephew of Sir James Brooke is rajah or ruler.

Here it was that we came across the delicious tropical fruits of the Indies, the mangosteen, the durian, and the custard apple. Strolling about one day, my attention was attracted by some round, reddish-brown balls, about the size of a common apple, with a slender stem, having at its base several close-fitting capsules or leaves, scattered along beneath my feet. They were so artistic, I gathered some out of mere curiosity. Finding them too hard to separate, I drew the blade of my knife across the thick outer covering, having to use as much force as in opening an oyster. This shell grated against the blade like dried leather, and refused to be removed, so I with some awkwardness cut it quite in halves. The mangosteen is largely hollow, but right in its centre, clinging to the upper and inner terminus of the stem, were several little creamy-white sacks, which entered my mouth so quickly there was no time to think either of malaria or poison. But ah, it was like nectar! The durian, at full ripeness, however, has a fragrance peculiarly its own, to which onions and garlic are roses in comparison. It also has a strong, spiky husk, and, should one happen your way, with only the force of its gravity from an overhanging bough, you would be surprised at its forcible impression and the length of time you bear it in memory. Pepper, cinnamon, clove and nutmegs, are among the common exports here, and the rhododendron, pitcher plants and orchids smile upon you everywhere.

The original people are the Dyaks and Malays. The Dyak is a little larger of the two, but though intelligent and truthful beyond many in our own land, they have little or no education, name the months as first, second, and so on, and measure hours by the sun's height from the horizon. Distances from Sarawak to points in the East are also measured by the same process, it taking the native the time indicated by the sun's position to travel to a given place. The Dyak expends little for clothing, the men using but a narrow waist-cloth of red or blue cotton, and the women seem content with something of a like nature, only descending further towards their knees, but often as scant and as awkward an impediment to easy progress as that of their white sisters in America. The blow-tube and spear are still in use as weapons, and the bird or monkey is generally doomed, if the tube is once raised to the mouth, or the javelin leaves the hand. But I am forgetting that my object is to merely outline, not to give a detailed account of my trip, so let us aboard and cross to the southwest. The monsoon is awaiting our coming, but struggles with us but a day. We pass three large islands, all uninhabited; Point Varella; the Ass's Head; and are within 100 miles of the equator. From my diary, I find that it was not the monsoon that most troubled me here, but no greater a thing than curry and rice, and that my Chinese servant was shocked at my persistence in refusing his much-prized peppery dish for this cunningly devised sweet meat.

It was not long before the low-lying coast of Lower Siam and the Malay Peninsula rose, like a silver thread, on our starboard. Soon, by my glass, long lines of beautiful palms stood dimly out on the distant horizon. It was not long before our whole view changed to mirrored sea and graceful palms. The land seemed to have suddenly disappeared and left the trees bathed in deep water. The whole scene was of more than earthly beauty. For hours no change came except our steady approach to the equator. Now and then a canoe or collection of thatched huts peeped out from between the foliage, and soon a Malay boat bore slowly down upon us. We paid it no official attention. Other boats, long, graceful double-enders, laden to the gunwale with rare sea-shells and fruit, soon followed as fast as paddle and Malay muscle could propel them, but the quiet of sea and sky, amid the vast wealth of palms and forest verdure, drove humanity quite out of mind. Ah, here at last was quiet and rest! Here, when a school-boy we read, roamed the savage man-eating and cruel torturing pirate of a Malay. There, within a stone's throw, in gracefully-constructed boats, as pretty as the gondolas of Venice — and quite as black — with reddish-brown skins and attractive faces, sat their descendants. If those stories had been of the lower Chinese, they would have seemed more credible. I do not mean to intimate that we were unarmed. On every steamer, from Japan to Egypt, there was no end of breech-loading guns, cutlasses and small arms, and the wheel-house was always lined with them, but in all my trip in the Malay Archipelago they were scarcely given a thought.

But on we went. Miles after miles of low coral islands to the southeast and the northeast, some below the surface of the water, and none much above it, seemed to grow before our fascinated vision. From Horseborough Light-House to Java there was little change, though southeast of Sumatra the groups appeared the most interesting. Not to dwell on these two islands, as they belong to the Dutch and are changing their exports, much tobacco being raised at the present time, I will merely say this, that the natives were most courteous and hospitable, and the resident Dutch so kind and painstaking that we seemed to be always at home. Most of the merchants and planters speak the English language with pleasing correctness, and many a time have we found the native

MALAY HOME AT THE EQUATOR.

as amusingly proficient. Love for flowers and birds seems strong among the Javanese, and often while conversing, you will catch them feeding the chance bird or caressing the wayside flower.

In due time we entered Malacca Strait, and made for the Malay shore until we reached the old Malay Singapore, now under the control of Governor General Weld of the English Government. For the first time since leaving San Francisco we ran up to a dock and were able to land without hiring a native boatman. Long, pointed boats, swiftly propelled by large paddles, followed us up the channel and displayed every variety of coral, sea-shell and fruit in so tempting an array, that we ached to buy them all. A village, built on poles, perched as if on stilts before us, and at high tide so separated from the woods around, that no wild beast could attack, reminded me of Borneo. The beaches were lined with canoes, which now and then shot out over the smooth water with the ease of a bird. The air was heavy with the fragrance of spice and flowers. A long, level road, skirting the water, seemed alive with little two-wheeled carts drawn by a yoke of small white cattle, guided by a native Malay in some such a way as we drive the horse. The cattle all had long, clear horns, which swept upward and backward, and then with graceful curve to the front again, just as if their natural tendency to grow straight forward had been regulated by a force to the rear. The yoke was tied to the horns, or placed between them and a prominent hump on the posterior part of the neck.

The native, as lithe and as gracefully formed as a maiden, with long dark locks crowned by a long piece of colored cloth, arranged turban style, sat just behind his horned steeds grasping a pair of lines running out and attached to the nose of each animal. It was a strange sight. The Malay had nothing but a narrow cotton waist-cloth and an ear-ring for clothing, and as often as I saw them working on the road or transporting merchandise, it was hard to believe, on account of their girlish figures, that they were not women in disguise. Here I was, but half of my world journey accomplished, yet totally forgetful of the many long miles between me and home. As I look back, my gratitude, on thinking of the pleasure that this country and people so richly afforded me, is inexpressible. Wherever simplicity and honesty reigned, it was almost impossible to tear myself away. It was so refreshing from the so-called civilized life at home.

What Sir James Brooke was to Borneo, Sir Stamford Raffles has been to Singapore, and as I walked down its long and pretty marine park, his recently erected statue gazing out over the magnificent sea and waving palms, was the first object to attract my attention. "Sinhapura," or "Lion City," was first settled by the Malay and Javanese, but was, for years, little better than the haven of South Sea pirates. Since the English have made it the capital of their Straits Settlements, its miles of pretty shore have been utilized for extensive commerce. Just below me were the large docks of the P. and O. Steamship Co., and about the same distance from the New Harbor rose those of the Messageries Maritimes, the well-known French line. Besides these the Government own many also. The soil is a red clay, and as there are 169 rainy days during the year, we practically wore red shoes the whole stay. This was our only point of resemblance to the native, however. To present ourselves in a bright turban, a waist ribbon and one earring was too much for our courage. We had, too often, fought against prevailing style at home to willingly yield here. The women are slender, graceful and entertaining — when you can understand them. Besides the short cotton skirt, they use bright plaids for a sack that can easily be drawn up whenever it is desired to protect or conceal the face or head. Long loops of gold and precious stones hang pendent from the prettiest of ears, and diagonally through the nose, full as pretty and symmetrical, pierce long golden ornaments, often accompanied with a large ring of the same precious material, so that while her voice falls like the ripple of the wave, or the soft gush of a mountain brook, it does not overcome the tempting impulse of telling her she is nearly as vain as her white sister in the great, far West. But it would have been hard for even us so to believe, so we patiently forbore. Boys, as straight as arrows, were playing in the streets something like marbles and ball, but using a short stick instead of the usual sphere.

Wishing to visit one of the many pineapple plantations, we were one day invited into the country, and, while observing the natives at work, it was observed that they would often stop, open a little bag, no larger than the usual purse, hanging at the waist, and take therefrom a roll of delicate leaves resembling that of the mulberry, or the mulberry just beside the window at home, where I am now writing. Separating one from the rest, and taking from the same bag, a little tin or wooden box of a yellowish-white powder, which they transferred by the index finger in small quantities to the leaf, they quickly conveyed the whole into their capacious mouths. My host, observing my curiosity, thereupon opened his own mouth, and disclosed as pearly teeth as ever graced a woman; but what was quite as noticeable was the unnatural redness of the gums and inner membrane of the entire cavity. With wide open mouth, he slowly raised his right hand in the direction of some tall, slender and uncommonly smooth palms in our vicinity, and smilingly observed "That he." I looked again. Large bunches of bright red berry-like nuts clustered under the leaves forty or fifty feet from the ground. It was the same fruit that had puzzled me on the Isthmus of Panama and in Borneo, but it was as plain now as the daylight. It was to them what tobacco is to the two-legged animals of the cud at home. It was the betel nut. The Malay, the Dyak, the Javanese and Sumatranese, the Bengalese and Madrasese, I never met without it.

The pineapple here appears to be longer and finer than those sold in America, but the stocks are no higher or stronger than elsewhere. As in the case of the betel nut, I was thrice otherwise pleasantly surprised in this place. The first time I set foot on shore we went on a long stroll. Long rows of cocoanut palms, now and then a cabbage palm, and still more rarely the magnificent fan palm, shaded our way, while here and there, floating in the high air, clinging in some mysterious way, were large clouds of purple, pink, yellow, and white flowers. The gorgeous beauty of the flamboyant tree, with its diversity of color, vied with the pomella and jasmine, and all with the bright red soil and velvety green herbage. From one of these yellow flowers is obtained our much-prized ylang-ylang perfume. Now and then a gutta-percha tree, a pepper, a nutmeg, aloe, or cinnamon tree, made its presence known, and, on the whole, the numerous fruits and nuts were as strange as the slight, girlish forms of the people. I had long become too weary for further uplooking, when I espied a moderate-sized tree clothed in large, peculiarly-shaped leaves, something like that of the oak, though many times the size. Pendent from its branches were a large number of oblong, and a little rough, green masses of fruit, which had come in my way before, but had been classed among the great unknown. To my great pleasure, my guide explained "Much eat." It was one of the most cherished objects of my voyage. It was what with meat serves for a rich, mealy potato, what with bread and milk becomes a toothsome pudding. It was the breadfruit of the Pacific, the cereal of many nations here. It was about the size of a child's head, and, were it not for the strange leaf, it would with great difficulty be distinguished from the large orange called the pomella, which equals the bread-fruit in size, but is in one variety more yellow inside, and in another a bright pink.

But let us to town. A broad drive or walk skirts the water for several miles. You pass two cemeteries with low monuments of round disks placed one above the other, or rectangular slabs inlaid with another of lighter and different material. Chinese joss-houses, Mahomedan mosques, and Pagan temples, streets muddy red, in which you must join the crowd if you will walk, for what seems like a narrow sidewalk is but the front of the native houses and workshops. But after being forced to join in with a funeral, a picnic party, and a religious procession, I decided, as my only way to a less exciting life, to try this covered sidewalk, if allowed. It was less muddy but, if possible, more crowded, so I had to walk sideways to make any headway, but the long rows of pomellas, melons, limes, pineapples, mangosteens, lichee, cocoanuts, custard apples, rambutan, duku, tapioca, beans, indigo, nutmegs, aloes, and every sort of trade in process, made it equally valuable and interesting. From temple to pagoda, from pagoda to mosque, no one disturbed my wanderings. Among the pleasant things about the Malay is the reproduction of natural objects in whatever he constructs for use or ornament. On the walls of his temples, one after another, in bare outline, rises the body, neck and horned head of his bellowing steed, and in the hands of the boatman or canoe man lies a palmleaf-shaped paddle, while his varied store of household goods and utensils interestingly increase the comparison.

The English here publish two or three papers, the Malay and Chinese one each. There is a public library and a large number of public hotels and churches, of which the Cathedral of St. Andrew, built in 1861, and located in large and well-shaded grounds opposite the park, is the neatest and most attractive. Quite near is a stone monument surmounted by a reddish-brown elephant, containing a tablet announcing the fact that it commemorates the first foreign trip of the King of Siam. The Chinese have many elaborate and even magnificent homes and grounds, many of them built with marble and porcelain tiles, on which are inscriptions of flowers, historical and pastoral scenes, the whole serving pretty much the same purpose as stone trimmings or marble in one of our modern brick edifices. The money-broker I found everywhere, tramping from place to place, from vessel to vessel, with a queer assortment of change in his long linen bag, and queerer ideas of business and gain in his red beturbaned head. Japanese yens would slide through his fingers at 2 rupees, 5 annas, and narrow silver bars, duly stamped with heathen hieroglyphics, rolled as swiftly away at 4 Rs, 5. It will not be the man's fault if he does not soon own the empire. Away he plies his nimble paddle, first on one side, then on that, till his sharp-pointed canoe seems to skim like a swallow over the wave, while his humble brother and the Chinese cooley get but 1-2 anna per basket for the coal, swung on their shoulders from a bamboo, they are hurriedly carrying on board.

For $2.00 we could purchase a whole dug-out full of pretty shells and coral. It is incredible how large some of these shells are. Were they capable of floating like wood, the naked little urchins about us would never have taken the trouble to burn out their present little sea-crafts. Here, as we are casting off to sail again, a score of these bright little fellows dance around in their light boats, calling out, "Sahib, Sarb, mister, say. One penny?" Or sitting patiently in hopes the penny may, perchance, come as a reward for good conduct. There they sit or rest on their knees, their little bare feet upturned to the sun's hot rays, and as white as your own, though the rest of their bare bodies are like bronze. Let a penny or a dime be swiftly hurled down to the sea, and presto! a score of heels suddenly fly up high in the air, leaving a lot of little boats and paddles floating helplessly away with the strong tide, and not a ripple left to tell of the whereabouts of the once merry group, now deep beneath the wave. You become annoyed, anxious, in fact, and are about to feel sad that you had encouraged their perilous sport, when up pops a forlorn-looking head, followed by blinking eyes and sneezing nose. Another, then another, till you count, with a long breath, the whole group together again. One has your penny tight between his glistening ivories, while he tries to give thanks and gain his fast vanishing boat at the same time. Up they climb, and with one roll they are inside again, and begin kicking or shoving their feet forward to expel the water, which, if very deep, is hastened by forcing the whole seated body pop-gun style, from end to end. As their lithe forms closely fit their pigmy boats, it works like a charm, but it is to be seriously hoped that the impinging surface is always smooth.

After turning over to a Sikh guard a large quantity of silver coin, we stood out into the channel, and had soon bid adieu to the joy of a lifetime in the fast retreating shores. Black fish, porpoise, shark, and cockroaches as large and abundant as mice, came around, as if to darken the memory of my past bright experience, till we reached Malacca. This is so like other Siamese places, we will not dwell. On leaving here we came to One Fathom Light, miles from shore, and then to Wellesley, with its grand cocoanut palms and magnificent plantations running down to the water's edge, and noble hills in the background. Fish weirs of bamboo, stretching out to the very channel, look like so many wrecked Malay boats. With a boom from our guns, we are at Penang.

An old fort, Dutch in appearance, lies low on a narrow level point, near which is the signal station. With my glass, away in the wooded mountainous interior, could be seen a shimmer of light from a high waterfall. As in holiday attire, in bright red, yellow and purple strips of cloth, dress-like wound about their waists, men, women and children flocked to our side. The Governor's yacht was close at hand, and both he and his secretary came into full view. We attended the national games, mostly athletic, upon the public common, and found several English and Scotch young men joining in the sport. Quite near is the Edinborough House, called after the Duke, who was here a few years ago and occupied it. The town seems quite flat, but is well shaded and ornamented with both palm and fern. Government schools, both for natives and foreigners, are here established, and English, French, German, Dutch and Indian vessels fill the harbor.

Wishing to see the interior of the country, which is as unbroken and full of wild animals as ever, an officer and I, taking "Beauty," who had climbed upon the rail and was making day hideous by fiercely barking at the native longshoremen unloading the vessel, hired a gharrey, a light cab with a small pony, to carry us as far as the road extended. It soon began to rain, a daily occurrence there, and the little animal began to suddenly stop now and then, and, vigorously shaking his shaggy mane, refuse all entreaties of his native master to go on. When he felt the rain subsiding, up popped his wild little head, as if saying "Ready, well then, just see me whiz!" he would nearly jerk our life out over the stony way. Passing the neat dwellings of foreign merchants, our way led through groves of cocoanut palms, with their heavy bunches of fruit ninety to one hundred and twenty feet high in some places, down to fifty or sixty in others, and native thatched huts interspersed between. Deep cuts, three feet apart, ran up the palm's smooth trunk, for native toes to climb in, when hunger or the desire of gain became sufficiently strong to excite his lazy limbs to action.

But at last the road came to an end, and telling the man to await our return, we posted off into the forest. Heavily laden ox-carts, coming from a neighboring quarry, were the first to greet us. Then a little boy and girl, with the innocence of childhood, ran and trotted along after us, despite the curling lip and marked sarcastic smile on the broad face of our quadruped guard. It made me tremble lest they should take it into their little heads to run along in advance, for, in the absence of all clothing, and the presence of a wicked idea in "Beauty's" busy mind, a serious disfigurement, if not dismemberment, would surely follow. A few pennies, surreptitiously thrown into their midst, had the desired effect of turning their curiosity to a safer channel and putting a stop to their advance. After a long tramp under our umbrellas, we reached a gradually ascending slope, containing nearly all the rare shrubs and trees of tropical growth. The rain tree which showers from its overhanging branches a grateful fall of rain, the traveller tree with its mighty fan-like leaves radiating from a common centre, and containing a quart of precious liquid for the thirsty traveller, the banyan, the areca or betel nut from which the name Penang arises, pepper, nutmeg and many other interesting trees grew side by side. The sensitive plant, with its little fuzzy pink blossom, crept everywhere under foot, and the maiden-hair fern cropped out everywhere. While resting after the shower, before undertaking an ascent of from 2,500 to 3,000 feet, I put my hand upon a small tree at my side for support. It was withdrawn most quickly, for I felt a host of many-legged insects at work on my arm. Freeing myself, a large nest of ants was discovered perched high among its branches. We had become accustomed to high-peaked ant hills on the ground, but were unprepared to find that all about us they had preempted the tree tops.

On setting out again, we observed "Beauty" suddenly prick up his cropped ears and wag his apology for a tail. His bow legs stamped the ground with amusing earnestness. We had come to a deep ravine sheltered by tall trees and luxuriant undergrowth, from which the dash and splash of water could be plainly heard. Neither the officer or myself had been on this mountain before, and were equally at loss to understand the sudden activity of our usually taciturn companion. We continued toiling up the steep slope, when, so suddenly as to make my heart leap, with a yelp, and a bound that sent the gravel flying like hot canister into our very faces, the bull-dog tore along up the mountain like mad. He had smelt game, that was sure. Then came a heavy fusilade from above, followed by a half-angry and half-frightened squeaking, that forced us both to laugh outright. This, then, was the free realm of harmless Jocko. We had heard, some little while before, of the presence of a tiger prowling in the neighborhood, and knowing the spirit of the dog, it had at first flashed across my mind that "Beauty" had made for him single-handed and alone. The cries grew louder and more frequent, as we hurried on. High branches and tree tops were swaying up and down as the nimble monkeys swung away from reach of harm, and slowly crawled along the larger limbs the scowling ape. Some, more bold than the rest, remained quiet behind a friendly bush or limb, and cunningly winked at us as we passed. The dog had stopped at the foot of a large tree and stood upright on his hind feet, baffled and disappointed. Not far in advance sat a large white baboon, the largest and the only white one I ever saw. Although a foe, it seemed as oblivious of the nearness of the dog, as "Beauty" seemed of him. We stood still, in fear that we should precipitate a rout, if not an engagement, but it was useless. On dropping on all-fours again, the broad-faced pup quickly espied his game, and, with bound and growl, descended upon it like a thunderbolt. He was too late, however. When he reached the ravine, the ape had slowly but surely swung out over and across, and being able neither to stop or leap the chasm — and if he ever had a choice, it was not like a bull-dog not to firmly seize and hold on to it — heels over head plunged the canine into the seething water below.

Actuated by kind feelings towards the brute, and not a little regard for our own welfare, for if it were discovered that we were responsible for his carcass running into the water pipe of the settlement a few hundred feet below, and thus depriving the warm and thirsty people of their only water supply for weeks, perhaps, and if his body became swollen, as it certainly would be, for months probably, we hastily made for the brink and looked down. It was an awful fall, my patient reader, but was it not an awful brute that had it? There, quietly seated on a large flat stone, his coat dripping wet, and a determined expression upon his not over-lovely countenance, was the object of our solicitude, looking straight up into our faces. Whether he was saying, "Did you kick me, sir?" or, "I'll fix you for this!" or not, we somehow regarded the look as ominous, and easing our consciences with the thought that his ingenuity was equal to an escape, and a shrill whistle, we departed. Near was a Malay joss-house, where we found a young man and maiden passing through a ceremony we understood was that of marriage. A large round rock, with a flat surface, had a fire thereon, and by its side some flowers and cakes, while a pair of gigantic brogans rested at its base. We were offered some cakes and fruit, and they went on their way rejoicing, while we still kept on until the old fort below, built in 1790, seemed a mere figure in the sand, and the large ocean steamers upon the water like toys. We had penetrated the wilds for miles, and ascended 2,800 feet or more on the mountains, so felt we had experienced enough to return. Not to speak of our frights and accidents, suffice it to say that we reached the steamer in time to see the Klings engaged in holiday games, and to hear that they could not be hired to work unloading the tea-oil, betel nut, and other cargo, until the holiday was over, as it is their only Sabbath or day of rest.

The native boats are borne along by paddles and oars, the latter of which are shaped like a round leaf tied to a long pole. The row-boats have painted, each side of their prow, large white or blue eyes made to resemble a fish. On each side of the Straits are miles of cocoanut-bearing palms, and large steamers are seen at anchor surrounded by native boats piled high with the nuts, which are constantly tossing from one to another till they reach the vessel's hold. The last of our pickled olives and Japanese apples were put on shore, and Governor-General Weld bid us adieu. We are told that his salary is $30,000 a year. He is to be succeeded by Smith of Ceylon. He has a pretty corvette, which carries several guns, close by. Our last thing was to take on some ice, which we got for $40 per ton. Pimento, allspice and the clove linger in my memory as I think of this, another fairy land, spices mingling with the mist of the 250 feet of mountain cataract far from the abode of man.

Glad to rid ourselves of the Chinese, who had reached the scenes of their next year's life, we were soon under way for Burmah, and then Calcutta, about 1,350 miles to the northwest. A shower followed us out into the Indian Ocean, and left us with a triple rainbow, impossible of description, so interwoven it became with the magnificent sylvan view of the Lower Siam coast. This was followed, in two days, by a hurricane, when we came to the Nicobar Islands. Here flint is still in use for axes and knives, and everything primitive. Here we met the Indo-China Steamship "Wing Sing." I now had a grand chance to study Indian life and human nature, for with the Chinese, all noise and confusion had ceased. A fair white-lady, with a little girl with long, bright ringlets, often joined me in conversation. They were queerly dressed and wore their hair parted low on the side.

There was a sickly white from Northwestern Hindostan, accompanied by a Malay wife of unusual beauty and timidity, and a little six-year-old boy, always in nature's own scant robes. A little gold ring in his left ear, and a charm of some sort on his left arm above his elbow, was his fullest dress, even to visitors, but never was a merrier child at sea or one on which a mother gazed more fondly. The father, seated on the deck with four or five companions in a circle, around a long, artistic pipe, half wood, half metal, with a long stem, which was passed from one to the other for a single whiff, seemed equally happy. This custom is common in India and Turkey. Several Siamese, with flower and vine-figured dress and turban, are going to Calcutta to dispose of their pouches of precious stones. Bright purples, blues, yellows, and red plaids flutter hither and thither as the men and women, so much alike in dress as to be almost indistinguishable unless you look up into their faces, flit nimbly by. Two Sikhs from Northwestern India are going home on a furlough, seven feet tall and with a form like Apollo. These are the famous Sepoys of the native English army.

One day we stopped to take two elephants, worth about $4,000, aboard. They were brought out in large native boats, but when alongside, the captain was at a loss how to load them. We rode high, and there was no way for the unwieldly animals to crawl into the port-holes. It seemed a dangerous as well as difficult undertaking. At first, the captain refused to undertake the loading, but, as the keeper was willing to save the company harmless from the result should it prove disastrous, he finally consented, first obtaining a writing from the owner to that effect. Bands of strong material were wound around the huge body of one of the animals, ropes attached, run through strong tackle, and the word given for the engine to start slowly. Just as soon as it cleared the native boat, it began to struggle and snort, and had to be lowered. Again the attempt was made, with like result. It was painfully evident that if the attempt were to be persisted in, some calamity would surely happen, if not to beast, to natives flocking around. A bullock can easily be hoisted by the horns, the powerful Roman horse in an iron-bound car, but the elephant is usually made to either walk or crawl in. Yet the owner insisted it could be done. Other bands were made, and with determined faces the signal to start was again given. As before, the powerful brute began to struggle, but less and less as it rose in the air, until not at all on the quick descent. The keeper and his attendants stood quietly by until the unfortunate creature came to the deck and with a few feeble struggles and gasps gave up its life, then throwing up their arms in frightful grief and rage, they loudly cursed us all.

Suffice it to say that the other animal went back to shore, and the poor, helpless carcass of his unfortunate companion went over the vessel's side, and we went sadly on. We had not gone far before we nearly ran into another waterspout, but we escaped the deluge only to fall into the hands of a full-grown cyclone, which sent us to Rangoon for safety. Burmah is very level here, with greyish soil, except in places, where it is more hilly, then it is red. Nothing in this attractive city, or in the whole country, in fact, interested me so much as the activity of its women, who, as in some French cities, seemed to possess all the intelligence, courtesy and brain of the place. Meeting several officers of the English army stationed there, my time was most profitably spent, but was soon on my way to Calcutta, the "City of Palaces," as it is there called.

The Burmese, Siamese, and Anamese, as far as my observation has gone, bear a resemblance to a mixed Chinese and Malay stock, and all dress in the brightest of reds, yellows, purples, and blues, in styles of vine tracery, flowers, and object design that would set an American girl wild. All wear a scant half dress, if anything at all, and if there is such a thing as trousers they must be a very abridged edition, and known only to a small part of the female class. They sleep, like their Northern near neighbors, on straw and reed mats, with a block of wood, sometimes constructed with a groove, for a pillow. Sometimes this pillow is made of leather and ornamented, and mats are found of quilted cloth, and in China, in addition to these, sleeping bags, or brightly-colored sacks, were seen.

John and his companions may be seen at all hours of the day reclining on his floor mat, with a tea urn, several tiny teacups, and some sort of cake or eatable on the floor by his side. Their language or tone is more uniform than that of Chinamen. The latter are amusingly peculiar in tone and inflection, and you must keep out of sight, as from a frog pond when curiosity or amusement leads one to draw near, if you wish to listen to a genuine colloquy, and to which, in fact, it bears closer resemblance than anything else I can imagine. It certainly is a satisfactory illustration of their dialectic voicing.

Their musical instruments, and tones as well, so far

exceed the wildest imagination, one must see and hear —and go mad—to form the faintest idea. The first Japanese music I listened to was on the streets of Tokio, and was well rendered by one male and one female voice, accompanied with two instruments similar to the guitar. The first Chinese effort in that line and in their native land, was from a group—call it orchestra if you will—consisting of two men, each with something like a long, crook-necked squash made of wood, with two strings running from top to bottom, and within a light frame, which we will, for want of a name, call a bow; another man with a large, round disk of prepared skin fastened to a wooden frame, which, seen elsewhere, would have been nameless—call it a banjo —and still another John with a tripod, bearing on its top a helmet-like metallic cone, with a protuberant, hollow wooden box. The only other participant was a celestial maiden of 17 years or so. When the music began, it was at a signal from the man at the metallic cone, who commenced tapping first the metal then the wooden box with a pair of sticks held between his fingers. Miss John thereupon jumped to her feet, with her chin prominently elevated. Another tap, and all went in for all they were worth. String rasped and screeched in highest key and most discordant tones, banjo trummed and dummed, as only a loose drumhead can. The tripod gave alternate sounds of uncertain click and dub, and amid the wild din and jargon, rose the female voice in high, discordant yelps. Nothing in my after experience even approximated to its weird effect, unless, perhaps, the midnight cry of the India jackals.

"If music is the food of love, play on!"

We were surprised early one morning by low-lying islands hundreds of miles out, one of which possessed a lighthouse. From the chart we found them the Andaman group. A steamer with government supplies was winding its devious way, and seemed the only sign of human life, yet palms, here and there, nodded their shaggy heads, and we were told they were covered with valuable timber and dye-woods. It had surprised me, when in Anam and southern China, to find the country so destitute of the magnificent forests found in the same latitude in Central and South America, but altitude and climatic differences probably are responsible for this.

Away south, above the Indian Ocean, the sun, interrupting, is building a massive arch of color, while, as from the dark storm-clouds, a wild sea fowl flutters down upon an isolated davit directly before our eyes. In my pleasure, I pointed it out to a Philippine Islander, who was one of the quartermasters. He ran quickly from the bridge where we were seated, to the bows, and silently creeping beneath the unconscious bird, with a quick and high bound, grasped it by the leg. It seemed cruel to take advantage of even an animal while seeking protection, but without a second thought, he had quickly returned, wringing its neck on the way, and presented the lifeless body at our feet. The constant warfare between man and the dangerous wild beasts here in Borneo, Sumatra, Java, and the Malay Peninsula tends to keep the natives unmerciful toward all wild creatures. The ape, ourang-outang, a species of wild elephant, panther, tiger, and rhinoceros infest all these countries, the only difference between the latter being two horns upon the Sumatran instead of the usual one.

For some days, while crossing the Bay of Bengal, we were constantly uplifted by an irresistible southern swell, indicating cyclones far south in the Indian Ocean. Twice a day the heavens were adorned with the brightest rainbows, and the broad, golden path of the rising sun was hardly less beautiful than the silver pathway of the full evening moon. It was now that I applied myself more diligently to the study of the Hindostanee, so that I might not be entirely dependent in mid-India. Spanish had been my aid in the countries and islands south of the United States, and French, English, and pigeon Japanese and Chinese, to the present, but in the immense country I was approaching, if I journeyed far inland, it seemed necessary for me to master a little of the language. After the study of Hebrew and Sanscrit, such a language comes pleasantly, and the peculiar position of the qualifying words, alone, seemed unusual or strange.

At 4 A. M. of the day of our arrival, we were met by a fine, trim-looking brig, containing Mr. Lindquist, our pilot, and soon saw the low coast of Hindostan, hardly distinguished from the sea. Two hours after, we were off the first lighthouse, on our starboard, where we put up our signals to announce our arrival, which information was immediately sent miles up the river to Calcutta. When up a short distance, we passed the SS. Port Jackson, from Melbourne, with her two decks crowded with horses. We then signalled again to what seemed an old castle, but what really was a government station and magazine. We were then near the southern shore, which for miles inland lay flat and nearly on a level with the river. It is dangerous to life, and seas have often swept across this plain, carrying everything living and movable, even to the strong, granite signal stations, helplessly before it. As I write, it is as green and fertile in rice fields as Japan, being all alluvial soil brought down by the river from the heights miles above. These immense flats constitute, with those on our starboard, the delta of the Ganges, the sacred river of the Hindoo. It is a pity the river is no cleaner, for a religious stream should be pure, if nothing else, but here on my right is a poor, little, white cow floating out to sea, its poor, swollen body begging for burial. The Hindoo kills no cow or bullock, nor buries them. He does not always bury his family or relatives, but often packs them off in a field or on a high scaffold, as they do in Borneo.

Following after the cow is an object so human that you will believe the stories of the early English settlers in this country, who had to use and often drink this dirty water, and who often pulled up in their buckets all that is mortal of a dark-skinned infant. It is fast going out of practice, however, for the English magistrate before Lord Ripon's day, set his foot down with an emphasis the native dared not misunderstand. Lord Ripon's memory is more grateful to the native than to the English here, for he made the innovation of having native cases brought before native magistrates, a policy which can work no harm and a great deal of good, as long as honorable men fill those positions. Along the banks are tall weeds and feather grass waving in the breeze, and, now and then, clumps of something that resemble the willow-tree diversify the low inland view. Soon native huts, with long, canoe-shaped roofs, covered with seed and grass thatch, appear near the shore. Hundreds of long-horned cattle are peacefully feeding in fields dotted here and there with high stacks of rice, straw and hay. In fact, going up upon the tide, is something so like one of these stacks, that it is not until you get opposite and see a long, dark form perched on its top and grasping a long steering oar, that you perceive that it is controlled by a boat beneath. A British-India steamship, followed by one of the Austrian Lloyds, was then passed, and we began to see more of the vast agricultural system of the country. Solid monuments marked the irrigation company's boundaries, and cotton, oil and indigo began to appear in vast quantities.

Leaving the mail at Diamond Harbor, 30 miles below Calcutta, with which it is now connected by rail, we passed on once more up the stream's tortuous channel. Daily bulletins are required from and to every pilot navigating a vessel through, as quicksands and changing bottom constantly threaten the navigator with destruction. At the James and Mary, we passed a British-India steamship, with nothing but the top of her masts visible, having gone down by running into quicksand that was supposed to be far above. Quite near is a Hindoo village, consisting of the long, haystack-looking huts, with low doorways, hardly any windows and no chimneys. Conspicuous in its midst, however, is a much higher edifice, with large dome and several spires, apparently of stone construction. This is the first Hindoo temple on native soil, brought to my notice. It is quite at the river's edge, with a grand expanse of green rice fields extending miles into the interior. As I look at the people and then at the sunken steamship, with its undisturbed cargo, it is with wonder that they do not all turn wreckers, but superstition here has often greater protective influence than force of arms, even. It is strengthened, in this case, perhaps, by the fact that a companion boat of this line, a short time before, was caught near the mouth of the river in a cyclone and went down with a loss of 750 lives.

Directly in front of us, is a small steamer, with a broad, double-decked flat boat on each side. They are full of merchandise from these rich fields, but like a trio on our city sidewalks, if you wish very much to hasten, the slimness of the man or the breadth of his two female companions hardly afford the necessary patience for a stoppage in transitu. Reeds, feather-grass, cotton and sugar-cane, gracefully waving to and fro, are now becoming more abundant. Native dinghys, like a lance-shaped leaf folded longitudinally, shoot up the turbid stream, while to the right, with joy the stars and stripes of the "El Capitan," the "Granger," of Boston, and three other vessels, moored off a cotton factory, are discovered. If memory serves me, these were the first vessels under our flag met between Hong Kong and Hindostan, but it was sufficient for the pilot to remark, "The finest sailing-ships in our waters used to hail from the United States, but times have greatly changed since I came here, 40 years ago." They were noble looking boats, as few as they were, so the point of his statement was somewhat blunted. As I write, the "Farragut," of Boston, one of the largest sailing vessels in the Boston and Calcutta trade, has been so long on her return voyage as to excite great fears of her safety. She has probably met the cyclone of the Indian Ocean, so fatal to shipping. On the Southern bank, we now came to large pyramidal mounds of brick, which were awaiting shipment, indicating an industry of large proportions. For miles they were constantly in sight. Soon substantial residences came in view, the tops of the Botanical Garden on the left and the Zoological Garden on the right. Next, a native with a long wand, from one of several neighboring roofs, aroused countless pigeons to the great annoyance of a large bear nervously walking his cage in a corner of the grounds, and several other animals scattered along the bank. A high, open-work fence surrounded this group of attractive residences, which appeared to be Government buildings.

Here is kept the King of Oudh, whose realm was on the Ganges, just northeast of Benares, which included historic Lucknow, and contained more rural population than any other proportionate part of the world. An annuity of 12 lakhs of rupees was, some thirty years ago, settled upon him for the loss of his province, but as he refused to sign desired papers, he was brought down to this remote spot, where he is supposed, for want of other employment, to rule over his hundred or more wives. A hard task, no doubt, but probably much needed. Needless to state, that with him expires the title, and all government aid to his household. Wajid Ali Shah is no longer a young man. In a very few years he will be gathered to his fathers.

As on we slowly passed, we saw the ship "W. H. Lincoln," of Boston, lying at her moorings, and Fort William, with its fine green lawn, just beyond. Next in view came the large Court House and Municipal Building, and the Maidan and Dalhousie Park with its drives, walks, bath and statues. Suddenly a bird settles down upon the rigging. Another and another follows, until their presence and occasional "caw" are annoying. The sky seemed thick with them, and as one boldly walked up and nodded to me from the rail, on inspection I found him very similar but less black than our crow, and with a light-brown ring about his neck. But like the buzzards of America, how can they tolerate them! In the interior, you will, with alarm, suddenly come across a long-legged, large-bodied and big-mouthed creature which you may surprise, seated with his pipe-stem legs stuck grotesquely out before him; or which may meet you, if you are small and timid, with his long bill wide open, as if just eager for business. This is the adjutant or gigantic crane, like the raven, sacred here, and which, with the midnight jackal, feed on carrion and do good service as scavengers of the streets and streams.

But here we are at last, within thirty feet from the ghaut or landing, moored to two immense iron buoys by chain cables. If we go ashore we must signal and hire some of the many native boats, which by the hundreds line the shore. It is done, and one with a high awning is quickly alongside. You must be careful, or a misstep will cost you your life, for the undertow is so strong that expert natives often lose their lives here, in full view of hundreds. Once on the paved bank, I turned to the Hindoo and gave him a silver rupee, whereupon he carefully counted out and handed back a full rupee in change. This left me as much in doubt as before as to what fee he should receive, so I gave him some annas and left him perfectly satisfied, a thing that rarely happens in England or America. Another thing I noticed, a few minutes later, while passing along the crowded streets, that the native touched his cap or turban and courteously stepped aside for me to pass.

Tall men, whose swarthy bodies were bare of clothing, except a yard of striped cotton cloth gathered around the waist and reaching to the knees, with large goat-skin bottles strapped to their backs, trotted along whisking before them the cooling spray alike on parched earth and thirsty man. It was nearly evening, and the Maidan was fast filling with English and European turnouts. It was not long before it became a veritable Hyde Park, where all London delights to take an airing. Many a time I have sat on the iron chairs at Hyde Park Corner, and watched both horsemen and equipage, the Princess of Wales and family, and others of like note, but the scene cannot begin to compare with the Maidan, with the soft, fleecy softness of the eastern dress, and the rich reds, purples, and blues, of the native costume. In fact, the symmetry of form and loveliness of feature among the women and children, and often men, of India are remarkable. How much this has to do with the practice of keeping the wife in seclusion at home, or in hot, stuffy palanquins when traveling, is problematical. But as this is generally confined to the upper classes and caste, and, in fact, is slowly going out of practice even among them, there is no great obstacle to a general study of them all.

This general seclusion of the women has, of late, given rise to many interesting social and moral questions. The European and American female physician, clergyman, and missionary, with the idea that medical science and the Christian religion would add to the welfare and happiness of this apparently isolated sex, have zealously worked against this strong caste custom until, in some instances, they have gained way to their presence.

Closely connected with this seclusion is the custom of infant marriage. From the time of Manu, some three thousand years ago, it has been the custom, as a part of the Zenana system, to early choose a child-wife for each male youth. Neither can then realize either the duties or responsibilities of their true relations, and are kept apart for years, and constantly taught, meanwhile, to love each other, pretty much as we encourage our children to treat each other kindly. To this is added the idea of mutual duty. Thus, it would seem the sense of duty would be more active than the emotion of love in finally drawing the pair together. Yet, there is an inner beauty to this system of marital teaching. It leads the infant mind and heart to love, honor, obey, and perform all those little acts and offices that, when sincerely and gently done, make man's life and the lives of his children attractive and lovely. Thus, when the awakening to a realization of their true relation dawns, the early training towards duty makes infidelity, separation and divorce, that fast-growing hydra of modern society, next to impossible.

The Zenana system teaches the wife that home, not the street, flirtation and gossip; that her husband, and his children, not those of any man she may happen to fancy more, need and claim her undivided time and attention, her kind and gentle ministration, and her hourly love. Peace and harmony thus prevail in the humblest home. There is no seeking to become conspicuous in conversation, dress, or public office; no craving after immediate acquaintance with every male stranger that appears well dressed or drives a fast horse. Modesty, purity, and gentle sincerity make her the idol of her home, a creature worthy of her husband and her Maker, and often a model for the very men and women sent to convert her.

As might be imagined, the first thing next to ascertaining the whereabouts of Lord Dufferin, who at the time was the Governor General, at a salary of $125,000, search was made for the Black Hole, where, according to Mr. Holwell, on June 20, 1756, one hundred and forty-six persons were driven, by the command of the Nawab of Bengal, into the guard-room of Fort William, a place hardly twenty feet square, and with but two small windows, and all but twenty three perished before the next morning. Mr. Holwell was one of these survivors. I have called it the guard-room of old Fort William, though it is my own conclusion, drawn from these facts. To my inquiries as to the location of the Hole, I was told by several that it was located on the spot of a certain government building, and by others that it was enclosed in Fort William. As the present Fort William was not constructed until after 1756, and by Col. Clive, who had come up from Madras to punish the natives, and that, too, farther down the stream, and as, also, there was, at the time of the massacre, an old Fort William where now the custom-house and other government buildings stand, my conclusion was that the spot is now beneath the latter buildings or warehouse, and not some distance down the stream, within the present fort.

Of course, the disappointment is always unpleasant

in not finding the identical thing you seek, but memory brings up a like experience in hunting for the Bastile on my first visit to Paris. Up and down, and down and up, the fruitless search went on, until it suddenly flashed across my mind that, possibly, it had never been rebuilt after its overthrow by the Commune. On this theory, the old site lay right before my eyes all the time in the Place de Bastile. My theory was right there; I believe it right in regard to the Black Hole of Calcutta, now. The Government House, the official residence of Lord Dufferin, is opposite the Park, and clearly in view. Lord Dufferin and lady are deservedly popular here from their many reforms and kind and benevolent deeds. Horse-cars run through a portion of the city, the fare being so many pice, a copper coin of less value than the silver anna. The European quarter is now well marked from the thatched huts of the native population, and many of the causes of malaria, once so prevalent, are effectually removed.

As I pass along the streets, many scenes, common to the interior, surprise the eye. Some have curved or straight white or red lines, or sometimes dots, chalked on cheek or forehead. Here stands an old man with palzied arm pointing stiffly into the air, and most wretched face, to whom all natives seem to offer alms or obeisance. He is a priest, or holy man, whose long abstinence and penance, perhaps, has reduced him to this mere skeleton, and, at the same time, raised him to honor in the estimation of these queer people. The arm was, I am told, reduced to its helpless condition by holding it piously on high. There was a time when the native manifested his devotion by a journey to Benares, crawling the hundreds of weary miles, like a caterpillar, depending upon the fields or chance charity for sustenance, and often sacrificing his life to the prowling panther and tiger infesting every part of that region. Now the Church of England, the Baptists, and other Protestants, besides Mahommedans, Catholics, and the Order of Jesus, are all, in their way, working upon and against the Brahmin and Buddhist priests, and have here many schools, commodious churches, and one cathedral.

It is not uncommon to meet people tattooed down to their very knees, while others are fairly loaded with gold and silver necklaces, armlets, bracelets, anklets, and toe-rings, and it is truly a rich sight, when in immediate contrast with the delicate laces and white, fleecy costumes tastefully arranged upon their healthy, graceful forms. It is also common to see trained animals upon the streets, and even on the river, eighty miles from its mouth, were observed in the very midst of the family, and in a dinghy scarcely sufficient to give standing room, a deer, an ape, and a bear. There is one thing for congratulation, and that is that the same weather which covers us all with a perfect sheet of perspiration drives the untidy from tom tom to a bath. Every morning, the Ganges and its tributary, the Hoogly, are lined with men, women, and children, up to their waists in the cooling though dirty water. And in the interior, not only people, but groups of buffaloes are seen, the latter up to their very muzzles. This animal, yoked to a rude two-wheeled cart, is a common sight. Its broad feet make it superior to the horse, or even the ox, for marshy places, and, once in use, it goes everywhere. Its immense semi-lunar horns are a terror even to the panther and tiger, whether in a wild state or on exhibition. In addition to the river, several canals furnish the Bengalese with water, and new baths are building inside of the Park at Calcutta. Noticing a long line of natives with bright brass or copper utensils file along early one morning, I found that they stopped at an ornamental watering fountain, erected, according to a tablet, by the Prince of Wales on his recent visit. It was free, and, for that reason, the people truly appreciated it.

While Benares and Calcutta are old and large cities, no worthy bridge at these points spanned the Ganges until the year of my visit, the jubilee year of Queen Victoria, who now also is styled Empress of India. The bridge is in the nature of pontoon or floating bridge, but well accommodates the public. India has now its railways, the one from Calcutta to Bombay being 1,400 miles in length, and runs through the wild midlands. It also has many fine viaducts. Among the most remarkable sights are the temples, hewn in solid rock, but as dak-gharries are the usual conveyance away from railroad lines, they are not easily accessible. Strictly speaking, they are Cave Temples, and abound with paintings and sculptures, and are decorated with bright frescoes. They seemed to be confined to no exclusive part of India. The Ajunta, 32 miles only from the Great Indian Peninsula Railway. The Caves of Ellora, 40 miles from Nondgaon, of great antiquity, has a chamber 180 feet square, and in its inclosure are two obelisks 80 feet in height, with a base of statue of an elephant, all carved and hewn from solid rock. On the Island of Elephanta, six miles from the Western Coast of India, and near Bombay, are three such Cave Temples, one 133 feet by 130, and 20 feet high, supported by immense pillars finely ornamented. A three-headed bust of gigantic proportions faces the entrance. It is supposed to represent the Brahmin Trinity. The island derived its name from a solid stone elephant 13 feet in length, which has now disappeared.

In travelling in the interior, one should carry his bed and bedding, for at the Dak-bungalows nothing comfortable is found. The use of one of these homes costs about a rupee per day. You pay extra for food and other accommodations. Taking into consideration that you may have to ride pig-a-back or in a covered bullock cart, and have to wait for hours for even this quaint and dislocating conveyance, travel in the interior with food, utensils and bedding, has but few attractions. If you *must* see a wild tiger, bear, elephant, panther, crocodile, buffalo, or deer, it is better to journey up and down by train, where you are safe, and see them on the move, as is often possible. Allahabad is interesting for the size of its tamarind trees, with thousands of flying-foxes, and two Pali inscriptions of great antiquity like those at Delhi and Benares. There is also here a banyan tree, said to be 1,500 years old, the resort for the devout from all around, as it is the sacred tree of the natives. To once worship here and bathe in the neighboring waters of the Ganges, no journey can be too long or fatigue too great. It is here, as I have said of Calcutta, that you see long-haired and almost nude men covered with dust and ashes, looking like human skeletons, the Fakirs or holy men, for which the native, unaccountably, except from superstition and ignorance, professes respect and the deepest sympathy.

But before it escapes my mind, let me say a word about this tree, so singular in its formation as well as so sacred throughout India. It commences a single stem or trunk. Soon branches shoot out. From these branches long filaments or air roots descend towards the mother earth. The native tenderly cares for these until in its downward growth it is trained to the ground, where it soon takes root. Instead of one trunk you now may have several, while at the same time the first trunk is rising higher and sending out more limbs which, in turn, are sending more filaments to the ground. One is on record with a circumference of 2,000 feet, containing 3,000 trunks, and capable of sheltering 7,000 people. There is one in the Calcutta Botanical Gardens of similar grand proportions, which, with its heart-shaped leaves and thick foliage, is truly worthy of the name of the Temple of Nature. The poorer huts generally have above them the graceful tamarind tree, but on their days of religious devotions, which may last a whole month or more, during which they toil not, neither do they spin, despite the threats or curses of Europeans, they hie themselves away to the grateful shade of the banyan. I am sorry to say also that, although holy water and the priest are gaining strong foothold among these men, the use of fire-water is spreading faster, and that, too, imported from civilized countries.

Another strange place is Deogurh, where 100,000 pilgrims annually arrive at its temples, and then go on to Puri, where are the temples of Juggernath and the idol of Vishnu. Wishing to see Mt. Everest, we found we must go to Darjeeling, 379 miles from Calcutta. It is 7,169 feet above the level of the sea, but is reached without any great fatigue. This is accounted for by the exceedingly attractive country through which you pass. Long stretches of poppy, indigo cotton, and tea plantations lie at your feet, while away in the distance rise noble heights of 25,000 feet, supported by the kingly Mt. Everest with 4,000 feet of head and crown additional. While on the way to Benares, one can stop and visit the Monkey Temple, infested by hundreds of these queer creatures, all clamorous for food and attention.

Benares is but 475 miles from Calcutta, and contains about 200,000 souls, a greater part of which are Hindoos. You are constantly reminded of this by meeting at every corner a vermilion-painted deity, so grotesque often as to excite laughter instead of reverence. Along the river-side there are some fine buildings and temples, though, as in Venice, some have followed their foundations to a dangerous incline, caused by the action of the river on the underlying soil. The houses are mostly of stone, and often of good height, but many of the streets are like those of Chinese cities, too narrow for anything but pedestrians. Besides 1,000 Hindoo temples, there are 300 Mohammedan mosques. In addition, every niche and corner, inside and out, contains a shrine for domestic and daily worship. The Bathing Ghauts on the Ganges, almost any morning, reveal most extraordinary sights and sounds, and the ascent of the minarets of the Jumma Musjid gives the whole city in all its beauty and quaintness. Working of brass and copper ware,

HINDOOS BATHING IN THE SACRED GANGES AT BENARES.

so commonly in use in India, is one of the chief industries of the place, and nearly as interesting as its justly celebrated cloths of gold and silver brocade.

But not to be tedious, let us pass Lucknow and Cawnpore, Delhi and Agra, which are deeply interesting in a historical and mineralogical point of view, and hurry back by rail to Calcutta, to the scene mentioned in my very beginning. The French steamer, under my old friend's control, swung around at the King of Oudh's palace, and we bid adieu to northern India. Hundreds of kites followed in our wake, rising high in the air and then, doubling their wings, shot like an arrow into the disturbed water to surely rise fish-laden. Dinghys, with long bambo poles supporting a large net, floated sidewise down with the tide. Each contained three or four natives, who, after allowing the net to remain beneath the surface a few minutes, quickly ran up the opposite ends of the two poles until their united weight overcame that of the net and catch of fish, and sent it high in the air. The fare, in a very short time, was transferred to the boat, and the net cleared for a repetition of the business operation. More curious still were the tactics of men standing waist deep and pushing before and around them a smaller net of about ten square feet, which, from time to time, was raised to the surface, and the catch, in a twinkling, transferred to a large turban on their heads.

Eighty miles down brought us to the great deep

again, far from men and beast, and face to face with the mighty forces of nature, the terrific cyclone and pitiless sea. While reading the Calcutta paper my eye caught upon the following: "SS. Paramatta, arrived yesterday, reports on August 9, the heat in the Red Sea was 190 degrees in the shade." Hitherto, whenever a thermometer was convenient, the highest range noticed was but 130 degrees, and that was about all I wished to bear, but the officers soon convinced me that such heat was possible at the time of year, a fact experience taught me to be true, when in my journey we found it 160 degrees in Arabia, in September. Indeed, from the time we left Calcutta until we landed at Alexandria in Egypt, it was so warm that the punkah was always kept in motion at meal time. The great heat had its compensation in our superior accommodations and fare, for which, as long as I travelled on this line, no praise can be too great. The entire after-part of the boat, which was elevated some 12 feet from the main deck, was protected from the sun and wind by a secure awning, and kept as neat as wax, so that, although dressed in plain white, we could sit down or recline anywhere without fear of injury.

The same can be said of our food. An abundance of courses of tastefully-arranged and delicately-cooked viands were, always courteously served by French waiters, who seemed to take pride in their success. And it was marvellous how many surprises a

French cook can pleasantly make, in but a few weeks' time. Dessert was the same, of which I recall the mangosteen, date, orange, and custard apple, with every kind of nut imaginable. Our officers, from commander down, were pure French. Our crew, Lascars and Seadee boys. It was a rich sight to see the Hindoo servants and waiters standing erect behind our chairs, with their solemn faces and queer life-preserver like hats, — for their heads were always covered in the saloon. Every one in the East has his body servant, so we had a number aboard. The term Lascar is generally applied to the native sailor or gunner, as the word Sepoy is to the native soldier. Which reminds me, that the noblest of the native army come from the northwest of India, and are called Sikhs. Seven feet in height is not at all uncommon among them. From that part of India I met a large number of people as white as I, though some had colored wives, which served to distinguish them a little from myself. In fact, I carefully refrained from any gift of dress or clothing to a maiden girl, using trinket or fruit instead, in the entire East, as to present a woman with her wearing apparel is quite equal to consent and minister put together in our country.

The second day out, of our pleasant company, Miss Dubern, Mrs. Atkinson, and the Pere De Wavre fell victims to the general enemy of ocean travel, but valiantly refused to go below, which fact, with its attendant free exhibitions of hurried, though covert, visits to the vessel's side, sadly gave the enemy the advantage over the yet unhurt. I busied myself looking at the flying-fish and attending to the children, while secretly aching for Mrs. Atkinson to recover, as she had promised to show me an ancient gold coin called the mohur, which she had found in Patna, and had preserved in the shape of a brooch. I afterwards, on her recovery, found it to be a very irregular, oval and thin gold disk, about an inch and a quarter in diameter, with strange bars and figures on each of its flat surfaces. It is a very rare coin, but, like everything made of native gold, is too soft for constant use. Many of my coins were equally interesting to the saloon. Col. Godfrey, one of our number, was of the 28th native Indian regiment, and, with his wife, was taking a trip for his health. Mrs. Godfrey was a perfect counterpart of an old friend at home, and, consequently, made the voyage one of rare pleasure. One day I caught them reading Mark Twain's "Life on the Mississippi," which would surely have given me a shock had it been anyone else. I had been so long away from everything American, it seemed like a blessing to see them enjoying even that overdrawn sketch of American life. Ah, those were happy hours, hours that came and went as though they were always to last! Dear friends, our sudden parting pains me still!

When we reached Madras, we found it impossible

to get inside of the breakwater, and that ten other steamers were in the same situation. This long stretch of solid masonry, erected at great cost, had been torn asunder and thrown helter-skelter by a mighty cyclone, so that it affords little shelter, if it does not really make navigation more dangerous While bobbing up and down on the immense billows, we saw the low coast and its attractive surroundings. A long street along a pretty beach has many fine buildings. Directly in the rear is the college, the church, the park, and to the south several massive government buildings. Wild billows chase each other from the broad ocean to the very street. No boat can live in such a surf. Natives are seen, wearing nothing but a medal, so to speak, paddling a raft of three logs, of which the centre one has a slight curve upwards, in hot haste for our patronage, and to our assistance. This is the historical catamaran, on which a native can carry the mail, when any other craft would go to the bottom. Their usual posture, when paddling, is on their knees, and often, when having fish or fruit for sale, the competition of these single-handed rafts is amusing. The skill of the Madrasese is no less remarkable than their courage, for I have met them away out of sight of land, fishing with nothing but these three small seven-foot logs, tied together with palm or grass rope, between them and a watery grave.

Next to the catamaran, as a surf surmounter, comes

the Marsula boats, large, deep, and bulky craft, fashioned by sewing long strips of board lengthwise together, as you would a ball covering, with grass or palm cord. One would as soon think of finding a calabash or cucumber-shell boat in use, as one sewed together in this strange fashion. But there it was, and full of silk, indigo, opium, and other exports, slowly approaching under the power of a dozen standing oarsmen, and a queer muffled figure, with a monstrous white turban crowning his dark features, urging them on. These oars, I noticed, were leaf-shaped at the blade, and rudely constructed as to the other part. Madras has two lighthouses, one at the fort, serving as an attractive ornament, and the other farther north. If it were not for these, it would be a treacherous coast, as the immense billows would swamp the stoutest boat. An irregular peak toward the centre is fortified with artillery, and is the only high land until you go north. In the park is a fine collection of wild animals. After seeing the beautiful situation of Madras on the broad ocean, one cannot imagine how so many prefer Calcutta, even in the winter, when the government is back again from Simla in the interior.

The natives live apart from the Europeans, which makes the settlement extend some eight miles along the pretty coast. It now ranks third as an Indian seaport. Col. Godfrey showed me his old dwelling here. These residences are usually surrounded by extensive grounds, laid out with plants and flowers, and are very different from his Burmah station. The leading street is called Mount Road, and leads from Fort St. George to St. Thomas Mount. The Cathedral and Mowbray Roads are also wide and neat. The latter has a fine avenue of banyan trees. In the square west of the fort is a marble statue of our old Yorktown friend, Lord Cornwallis, who once distinguished himself here. Near by is a fine equestrian statue of Sir Thomas Munro, by Chantry. His remains rest near by in the old English church, near those of the Missionary Schwartz. There is also an observatory here, from which all India takes its time. There are ten Christian cemeteries and many missionary schools. It also has a memorial to Bishop Heber.

After satisfying ourselves about Madras and its surrounding country, we put out to sea for the French possessions about Pondicherry, and soon saw its low sandy beach, pretty places and background hills directly before us. The beach is one of its prettiest features, but when you have been rowed a mile to shore, you find it as gay and interesting a place as India contains. A canal separates the native from the European town, and the real life of the place is some little distance inland. Near the water, however, is a large-sized statue of Gen. Dupliez, Nawab of the Carnatic, and once strong in influence at Hyderabad. Not far away, near the Boulevards, are many neat hotels, and as the healthiness of the climate and purity of its drinking water excel most seaport cities, it has the appearance of a gay and fashionable watering-place. Along the sandy beach, scores of happy couples wend their slow and joyous way, while a queer vehicle, not seen elsewhere, with large white sails and steered from within, moves up and down the same sandy course, giving invalids and children a merry boat-ride on solid land. The light-house rises from the square it ornaments, and not far from the only pier. The ten columns of native stone surrounding the Dupliez statute rise close by. The Cathedral has two square towers and a large dome, like the Notre Dame of Paris, and far to the North a Mohammedan mosque, with minaret and like dome, stand out in quaintest contrast.

In the interior we came across the most primitive money I had used, with the exception of the bar of silver before mentioned, and the cowry shell also used here in Southern India. It was a small oval copper disk with the rajah's stamp. The right to coin money is identical here with the right to govern, and consequently, when in the domain of rajah, marajah or nawab, you find and use their native coin. The English, however, have their own money in paper, silver and gold. Many of the silver rupees of the old East India Company are still in use. But a dozen or more of French women and girls are about to be rowed to the Tibre, so we might as well accompany them. Three mighty billows of surf nearly stand our boat on end, but when once beyond, the sea was almost glassy, and much too soon we reached the vessel's side. With three times three hurrahs, the boat crew left. We had hardly reached the deck, when still more enthusiasm was noticed from a boat containing a French consul and his numerous family. If Adele sees this, may she pardon this reference, for were there not six small persons besides herself? Ah, what an Adele! Who but you with your childish prattle could have consoled me for the loss of Col. Godfrey and his lovely lady, who had but then bid me a warm farewell!

With our eyes sadly fixed on the fast receding shore, over which we could still look into the pleasant country beyond, speechless at loss of friends, seen only perhaps beyond the vale, we watched the sun go down as on their graves. That night, out of sight of land, and exposed to crossing seas from the Indian Ocean, it was frightful. Ernest Brier, wife, and two children, had long before succumbed to the inevitable, and lay helpless. None but Mr. Lindguist, Mrs. Atkinson, and myself, were left on our feet, with Mrs. Atkinson on the doubtful seat, but still coming up smiling. After it became too dangerous above, we succeeded in forcing our way safely to the saloon, and there tried to cheer up the poor, homesick mortals then almost wild with despair. French nature is either very buoyant or despondent. Many were leaving pleasant homes for Tahiti and other distant fields of labor. Mrs. Brier, a lovely young woman, was, the livelong night, begging her husband to return, to only go back, and she would bear any hardship than endure the present misery longer. If joy has its heights, sorrow, none the less, has its dark depths of despair, and both may fall on the same individual.

Up, up, up, rises our gallant ship, when, in a trice, her nose is plunged deep into the raging billows, and struck, one, two, three, by the maddened sea, as by a mighty sledge. To say that my heart went out to those poor, helpless mortals, is unnecessary. Little Paul, a lovely, curly-headed boy of three, all night long loudly cried out for his helpless mamma, while six inches of water swashed around our feet in the cabin. Soon after daybreak we sighted the distant peaks of northern Ceylon, and saw signs of a quieter sea ahead, though huge white-caps, rising to an immense height, and often having their foundation knocked out from under them, struggled like aerial monsters all about us. None but the strongest vessel can outlive such a cyclone and sea. After passing Trincomalee, the sandy shore became higher, and mountain peaks appeared in the far interior. Passed both Little Bass Light and Great Bass Light, the latter a beautiful, flashing light, like an immense Oriental ruby. The next day found us, early, off Point de Galle, lying low and surrounded by hills, and is the most exposed point in all the Indian Ocean. It has a lighthouse and several large hotels and other buildings, but large vessels now shun its dangerous coast, and go on to Columbo on the western coast, where a strong breakwater protects them from both southwest and northeast monsoon. The nose of the Tibre rose on high and plunged straight down into the sea again about once a minute. Suddenly down swept a gale again and drove the rain before it till the scene was startingly like the drifting snow in midwinter. Every rain drop was lashed into foam, and upon the wildly racing billows appeared nothing but hillocks of ghostly white. The French Governor of Chandernagore, who had been unable to leave his stateroom since leaving Calcutta, must have thought that he had awakened in Dante's Inferno.

By the time we made Mt. Lavinia, the sun burst forth, and we were gratified by a sight of its fine hotel, with seven or eight miles of foam and surf, white, green, and blue, leaping high into the air. Away in the distance was the immense breakwater of Colombo, constructed in 1875, with a lighthouse at its farthest sea end, over which, in high, bold leaps, the same greenish-white surf was wildly vaulting. We were then grandly riding upon a beautiful yellowish-green sea, rising and falling like an egg-shell on its immense billows. Right before us, skimming along like a swallow, with a large expanse of white sail outspread, was a queer, long, narrow craft fashioned from a log, upon which was constructed, to the height of two feet, two box-like sides, and just space enough between to insert a slim pair of legs. Two seats, like those of any boat, ran at right angles across the top, and two long, curved poles, fastened at one end to the boat and the other tied to a long log running parallel to the keel, served, as an outrigger, to give it steadiness. It was a bom-boat, used here both for passengers and native traders. It glides over the water with lightning speed, cutting its way like a knife.

Far to the left were two high-walled, shoe-like boats with but one mast and a long, slanting boom with triangular sail, so ancient I knew that it must have come fresh from Egypt or the Nile. I had but to catch a glimpse of the long, red flag, with its crescent and three stars, and I was convinced. Ages have come, ages gone, but the queer Dahabeah, so familiar in Egyptian river scenes, has never changed. Above and beyond all, rose the majestic palm in countless numbers, with its usual accompaniment of native thatched huts peering out beneath. The Tamil is much spoken in Ceylon, but you find, as elsewhere in the East, a large number of Turks, Hindoos, Arabs, and Chinese. The first native I saw here wore his long hair, like a girl, fastened back with a large, circular comb. He was a Sinhalese merchant, and rode perched up in a bom-boat.

After rounding the breakwater, we took up our anchorage in the placid water behind. Boom-boom, came the outside billows upon the protecting sea-wall, rising in great sheets of foam and floating off in mist. At first I could not leave the spot, so grand was the display. The wall is constructed of 32-ton stone blocks, 16 by 20 feet, dovetailed into each other at an angle, and has a capping 12 feet above low-water mark. It extends hundreds of feet westward, with its outer end curving northward, bearing a light-house over which the monsoon constantly drove the beautiful billows up to the very land. Another light-house, containing also a clock, rises near the old fort and possesses one of the best and clearest lights in the world, a revolving dioptic, plainly distinguishable 18 miles. There are two little steam launches, but one is so asthmatic, we avoided it for fear that it might conclude, after getting us well on board, to give a last gasp and send us skyward. When on shore, we found the street soon led to finely shaded walks and cinnamon gardens. The long, peach-leaf shaped foliage is so fragrant that to-day, a year afterwards, those I brought home still give forth the delicate aroma. Among the palms, we found the cocoanut with its long spikes drooping with its load of from 12 to 20 heavy nuts, and the Palmyra, which yields from its flower spike many bottles of excellent toddy, the natives hanging bottles to it for that purpose for six months of the year.

Where the native lives on the cocoanut, he finds four nuts per day sufficient for support. Sugar and vinegar, as well as toddy, are made from the palm; also mats, thatch, and a substitute for cabbage. The taliput palm blossoms but once in a lifetime, and often after it is 60 to 80 years old. The blossom is 20 feet high. The sight of the cinnamon tree, flourishing in the white sand, is striking, as is the peeling of the bark from its tender shoots for commerce. Farther to the North coffee fields are numerous, but on account of the coffee-bug, tea is fast taking its place; and further yet, where still roam the wild elephant, buffalo, deer, panther, bear, anaconda, and cobra, were once fields of rare fertility and production, down to which, by a stupendous system of mountain reservoirs, dams and canals, water, ages past, had been conducted, to make it the "Garden of the East" that it was. There seems to be no coal, but iron is found in quite large quantities, and often in a state of purity. I was told that Sinhalese-worked iron is equal to the best Swedish metal. As you approach the harbor from the sea, you may observe a dark-blue peak far inland, like a monarch among the lesser heights. This is Adam's Peak, on the summit of which is a hollow, now roofed over, said by the followers of Mahomet to be the footstep of Adam. Hence the name. I need not add that the honor is contested; that the Buddhist claims it for Buddha, and Portuguese for St. Thomas. If I had made it, it would have been the same, except it would not look quite so much like that of a mule. I often on my trip indulged in creating foot-prints, hieroglyphics, and images, that the rare ingenuity of the Oriental mind may not weaken for want of subjects.

About here are found the blue, green, white and pink sapphire, cat's-eye, moonstone, and ruby. It was a genuine surprise to find sapphires like diamonds. It is not an uncommon sight to meet a native, in nothing but a waist-cloth, out of which he will draw a double handful of these gems cut, uncut, and set. The cat's-eye, although costing hundreds of dollars often, had for me but little attractions, yet the possession to the lucky native insures him life-long comfort and happiness. While examining the collection of a Mahomedan native, who wore on his head a little, tall, round straw hat, with bands of different color, and no brim, he became very social and disclosed the names of some of his recent customers, among whom were Eben D. Jordan and daughter, of Jordan, Marsh & Co. of Boston. Next to the gems, the rhododendron, which grows above the Sanitarium of Nuwara Eliya, interested me most. At home it rarely exceeds ten feet in height, but here a stem may measure three feet in circumference, and the trunk run to the great height of 70 feet, so rich is the moisture and soil of this region. Ebony and satin-wood are also found here. A cane of the former, finely carved and ornamented with native ivory, was here presented me. The head was carved to represent the wild elephant, and contained real ivory tusks. The country towns seem full of the finest carved ebony cabinets, boxes, and articles for ornamentation, for which they are justly noted. The pearl fishery is not of the importance in Colombo as formerly, but is carried on with great success just North in Persia. The manner of gathering them, however, was shown me by a Mahometan, who somewhat startled me with a remark touching his faith, little realized in Christian countries.

"You and I," said he, "are completely clothed in both mind, body, and soul. These poor creatures are destitute of everything. We believe in one and the same God; the number they worship is unlimited." I had just seen the old temple with its recumbent, giant god, refulgent in yellow and vermilion, and consequently could feel that there was some force to his succinct statement. Yet, even the missionary has to admit that modern civilization and commerce brings a grave change to these simple and true-hearted natives, wherever found living in the truth of nature. Many a time they have trooped by, garlanded with flowers, as happy and innocent as children, until I have felt commerce and modern society a curse. The truth is too apparent to the traveller, though ignorantly denied by stay-at-homes. Among the queer things you meet with here, are the geckoes, whose toes have pads with which they can climb perpendicularly, and walk on the ceiling, the white ant, or termites, and the walking leaf and stick. Ceylon was known to the Romans and Greeks, but the first European settlement was by the Portuguese, who started a factory here at Colombo, where the old fort now stands, in 1517. The Sinhalese kings induced the Dutch to drive out the invaders, which they did in 1656, and were in turn routed by the English in 1796. Kandy, now connected by rail, was the last to yield. The lash is here still used as a means of legal punishment, as I noticed in Singapore were the old stocks. Some of the natives speak Pali, which has been a dead language for above two thousand years. It is in this tongue that most of their valuable works are written, including the Buddhist Bible, called the "Tripitaka," which was written 309 B. C., and has eleven times the number of followers as our religion.

Its pure and simple doctrines still live in the native heart. By it falsehood, intemperance, anger, pride, dishonesty, covetousness, and taking even the lowest life, are strictly forbidden. Caste, here as often elsewhere, is but a social institution. Every trade is a caste, except among the Mohammedans. They have no caste. The Colombo Ice Co., manufacturers of artificial ice, used to declare a dividend of 60 per cent from two machines only, but tea and coffee raising now prove as good an investment for capital. The indigo plant raised here is a low weed with one stalk and flower. It is cut or pulled up and cast into cement tanks. After being mashed in water and submitted to pressure, the liquid is drawn off into another tank and filtered. It is then submitted to heat, when bright-colored crystals appear. Fully as interesting was the shoe plant, from which is made a deep purple dye. With this the Chinese women color their hair and eyebrows. It is also used for iron and shoe blacking, hence its name. Here I was forced to part with Mr. Lindguist, Mrs. Atkinson and others, with whom, in the common danger of our perilous voyage, so many impressive hours had been spent.

But my joy was great when, on first going aboard of the French SS. Volga, for Arabia, I found an English book lying on the deck. While casting some pennies to the nimble divers, who gather around as in the East Indies, I unconsciously spoke English, and was thus introduced to the owner of the volume, an English-speaking European on his way home from Java. I had become so tired of the mental exertion of using French, that I hailed him and a gentleman and wife, all with American faces but of Dutch birth, as an unusually good fortune.

NATIVE INDIA COINS.

CHAPTER VII.

*Behold what men hath wrought!
The soul of loveliness, a type of Heaven,
But once to mortal vision given!*

THE Volga was so inferior to the Tibre in pleasing style and raised deck, that I feared, with so many passengers, it would be unpleasant, but acquaintance soon obviated all difficulties. It should have been enough to have had Adele, whose constant laughter and limpid French was a sure cure for low spirits, and who came tripping down the wide companion-way into my very arms before I was hardly aware of her presence. I was not on a fishing excursion, however, neither was I in a mood to bite. Alas, I almost wish I had now! She had been to see Arabi Pasha, who lives here in exile, having the freedom of the town, but never venturing on the water. She had been to the cinnamon gardens and, would I believe it, had some of the fragrant leaves left. Bright, light-hearted Adele, how quickly seasickness stopped that eager tongue! To get you from my mind let me say, that red goats, as large as the little white cows of India, were about the last objects to appear in sight, flanked by eight Sisters of Charity just landed for Cathedral work. The Volga was on her return to Marseilles from China, and carried, among other things, gifts for the Pope's Jubilee, soon after held at Rome. Her deck was covered with canvas awning, and gorgeous Eastern ferns, flowers, birds and monkeys crowded its capacious sides.

With four men at the wheel and full speed on, we fairly danced over the water till we reached the low coral isles of the Maldive group, which shone with all the splendor of the opal. Here we moved slowly all one Sunday through their magical scenery. No steamers of deep draught thread the channel except by day, although it has a light. The islands are well wooded, but long lines of coral reef appear below the emerald water, making navigation extremely dangerous. Tall waving palms and low native huts were sparsely scattered along the coast, and for miles on our port, glowing beneath the midday sun with soft, bright colors, stretched the low coral beach. We had the piano brought upon deck and, from that day on, we were never wanting for a song, anthem, or even a polka. Besides, at every meal a music box, of almost endless variety of selections, lent spirit and zest to the flowers, fruit and, perhaps, flavor of our food. Every evening came a concert, to which all were prevailed upon to contribute, and often a dance, it making little difference whether the deck were level or at an angle of forty-five degrees. All was as innocent and harmless as child's play, and helped to give each day a joy and pleasant memory. We had a Japanese major and his general's son aboard who, like myself, preferred, at the dancing, to always play the audience, despite the constant protests and entreaties brought to bear against us. Perched high upon the stern-wheel box, not then in use, we dined on the fine green-skinned orange, the mangosteen, and various native nuts, pleasantly overlooking the happy crowd, and often tempting them to stop and partake.

Once, while so seated high and dry, an immense sea struck amidships and swept the rest of the men, women and children, like twigs, before it down to the opposite rail, where only the stout canvas awning saved them from a watery grave. All were drenched. My lady friend from Paris, Mrs. Bienville, her daughter, her daughter-in-law, and, yes, Adele, were as wet as drowned rats, and really looked about as attractive. Which, or how many, did I carry below? I forget. For days ran the same high peaks and deep, wide valleys of seething water, till it grew calm again, and seemed to change to a lighter green color. A silver-grey owl from the African shore, no doubt, came aboard one night and perched above the cabin door.

September 25, we reached Aden, the great coaling station for Australian and Eastern steamers. Now, again, the dug-out canoe appeared, this time under control of bushy-haired Africans and grey-haired Arabs, some, like the maiden lady of America, with a long curl hanging down in front of each ear, and all the rest of the head closely shaved. The Somauli from Africa were as black as the ace of spades, slender in form, and so economical in clothing as to wear nothing but a medal tied to the waist and a charm of snake-skin above the elbow. Happy Somauli, marching along erect as a pole, perfectly unconscious of the queer figure they were cutting, only intent on selling the Frank the long, tin roll reefed under their long, lank arms! In that long tin of about two inches in diameter, they shake out, before your astonished gaze, the finest, whitest, and downiest ostrich plumes that ever gladdened a maiden's eye. Arabs, with ibex horns, sword-fish teeth, peacock fans, coral, and even caramels of the purest gum-arabic and sugar, quickly joined the throng. The sight of their cotton dress-goods reminds me that I have omitted speaking of one of the commonest sights in India, and especially at Madras. It is the native travelling merchant with his bundle of rich embroidery and artistic designs impossible of description. Gold and silver thread is commonly used on velvet, silk, and other rich fabrics. Thousands of beetles' wings, humming birds' breasts, and glowing insects, are in this way utilized, and made to produce effects possible only to the Eastern imagination. The only criticism I would make, and a fair and just one, is the want, often, of symmetry and grace in their scrolls and vine tracery.

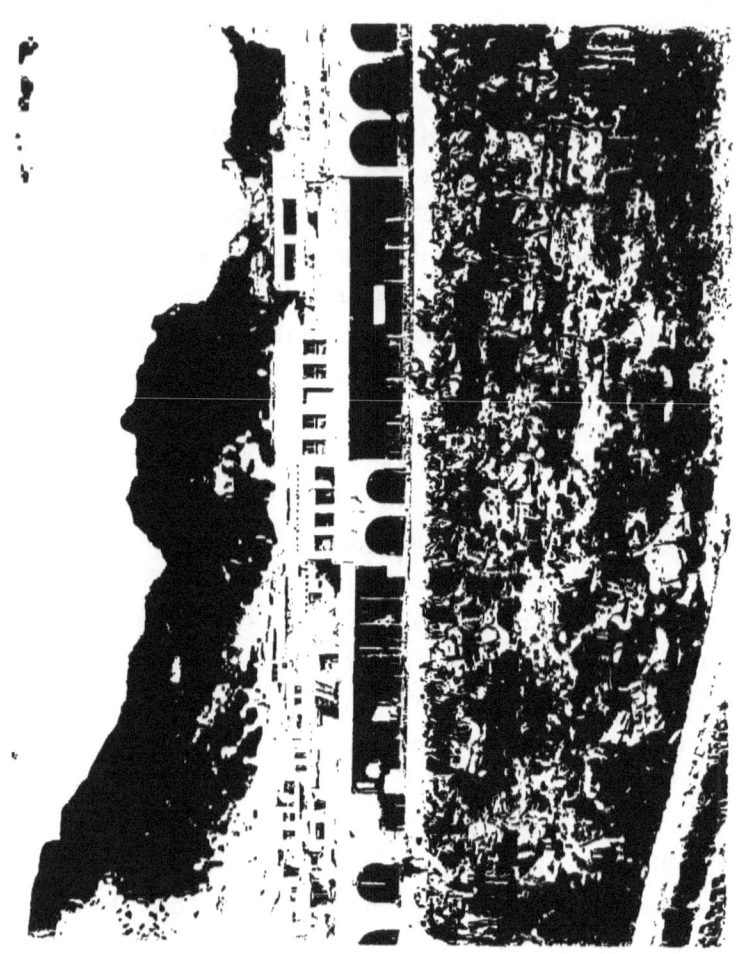

Not far off we see a band of men, with long, bushy hair standing almost out straight, as brown as the neighboring camel or the hot, parched hills beyond. The high slopes on the right are nude of vegetation, and resembled burnt gunpowder. They probably are of volcanic origin. The sun is intolerable, and the doctor forbade our uncovering the head, even at our meals. Does the thermometer falsify, or is it 160°? I am conscious of acute pain, as though a knife were entering the brain, accompanied with a strange, giddy sensation. We pass along around the bend, away to the north, and come to the old town of Aden. Opposite some queer, low buildings, reminding one of a Moorish town, is a square literally full of camels, some from Mecca, some from Persia. Some are resting on the ground, their long necks stretched at full length on the hot sand. Some are rising with a long, guttural groan, as if in protest of their load. Others are harnessed into rude two-wheeled carts. Everything but the houses appears to be suffering in the heat. Then on, on up to the elaborate and costly English water-works nestling high among the hills, and then gladly back again. Can Sahara, can Satan be worse! How mortals can exist here, say nothing of enjoying life, is a great mystery. They wear but little clothing, and their hair is so dry as to stand quite out straight. This, perhaps, keeps it from becoming matted and warm. But what of their nerves and brain? Is there an ossification of the one and the absence of the other? And yet, here they offer for sale exquisite workmanship in sandal and olive woods; but both of these woods come from afar, and possibly are brought here for sale. The peacock-feather fans, so prettily gotten up, may be native work, so the whitening of the ostrich feathers, but, at all events, you get a sorry idea of the Arab, as well as his noted, fleet and milk-white steed, from this burnt, forsaken country.

Later on, however, I saw some improvement, but have never been able to soar to a poet's view of Bedouin, Arab or Turk. Here, in Arabia, I was addressed as "Marster," (Master). In India, as "Sarb," (Sahib). Even among the rascals of Egypt, courteous expressions were as abundant as fleas, and nearly as pleasant. As in India, you hear a strange, reed-like music, and up from an innocent-looking basket at the performer's side, pops into your very face a wriggling cabra, or anaconda. Aden and the island of Perim are the English strongholds at the entrance of the Red Sea, but the strength of their fortifications is not apparent, though full in sight. The water is clear and full of fine fish, which, with some of the finest oysters ever tasted, helped us to a better view of the desolate town. While inspecting a Mecca caravan, I found some delicate lace, bead and fancy work equal to anything seen, but I wonder they do not invent something more appropriate for the head than their little, saucepan caps or, worse still, the massive turban.

Two pretty lights, one revolving in the Northwest, guided us on our journey out of this port, and we soon came to the Somauli Territory in Africa. Flocks of water-fowl and birds kept close to our boat until Massowah was reached. This was connected with the late Soudan War, in which Chinese Gordon lost his life. It has two islands near, and land lay on our port side for a long time. The whole coast along Abyssinia, Nubia and Egypt, is pretty much the same, a low sandy coast, with high barren land in the distance. I looked in vain for any claim the Red Sea might have to its name. A little red coral, a few red weeds, that was all. During the many days up to Suez, during which I coursed its entire length, it was as dark-blue as the ocean, and often as boisterous. At times, however, the intense heat from the great deserts on either hand forced the perspiration from every pore, and kept it in sheets upon the face, even when a strong breeze was blowing. It was the first time in my life of experiencing the strange sensation of feeling a breeze without the least evaporation or cooling effect. It was more like having very warm spray sent gently upon you. The sun each evening sank heavily down like a ball of molten lead, but the nights were glorious. Shower after shower of sparkling meteors shot down the clear, blue sky and, bursting, showered the air with brightest green, blue, and red refulgence. Many a night, from here to Italy, the planets gradually descended, as darkness drew on, until they seemed like red, blue, green, and yellowish-white lights swinging low on silver cords and sparkling in an atmosphere of pure hydrogen. Often was it repeated in Egypt and Palestine, and vividly brought to mind the night when the star arose over Bethlehem's plain. We saw also, here, the pelicans of the wilderness, pursuing, as of old, the even tenor of their way, in long, single lines against the sky. Nor must I forget the flocks of quail, also mentioned in the Old Testament. All are pleasant reminders.

Many steamships were here met, as the Suez Canal has entirely changed the line of commerce East. Formerly a few sluggish daharbeahs freighted with wheat or grain were all to be seen in the whole Red Sea. Now one is not surprised to meet a dozen of the largest-sized steamers with decks crowded with people, and hold full of everything the earth can produce. Suakim next came in sight. Here Italian men-of-war are having trouble with the natives, as Italy aims at holding this place at all hazards. When off Mecca, the sea arose in all its might. For the last time for days, this was a golden opportunity for seasickness, and every moment was thus industriously improved. I was glad of a change and, although far from being sick, I got my share of the bruises and bumps incidental to such a sea-frolic. A child cries loudly, and turning, I see its father has, in his course to the vessel's side, forgotten its tender youth and recklessly thrown it at my feet. You forgive when you see his lank form nearly bent double in his involuntary and frantic attempts at relief. That father and child were first cousins. I laugh at it now, but then it seemed a queer state of affairs in family relations. This man had an aunt, some thirteen years his senior, but really more prepossessing, and as she was so good as to have him, they were married. This was their first child, who seemed well and lusty in his privilege of calling his papa " dear coz," and his mamma " great auntie."

We were for days out of sight of land, and the sky all that time of a beautiful silver-grey, with the moon nearly as plainly visible by day as at night. We passed the light on the Two Brothers, when we were not far from Medina on the outside, and Assouan on the other. Now steamers became more frequent, and cheer after cheer, amid waving of handkerchiefs, went up from many a glad heart. Soon the extreme point of Ras Mohammed on the Mt. Sinai Peninsula, then its high, rugged, barren hills, burst into view. Next, land of Lower Egypt on our port drew equally near. Thus we entered the Gulf of Suez, on the extreme north of the Red Sea, which lay under the rays of the hot sun like burnished silver. With glass in hand, and steadfast gaze to the northeast, I awaited with nervous anxiety for distant mountain heights.

I did not have long to wait, for slowly upon the object-glass grew dim outlines of mountain peaks. Above and beyond loomed a craggy brow, apparently cleft in twain. No sign of vegetation, cedar, vine, or palm. The reflection from its glistening, arid sides caused my glass to lower. When I again raised it, almost opposite, grandly towered the object of my eager anticipation. A mountain monarch doubly crowned, in whose deep recesses man met and talked with the living God. Is there in all biblical literature an object so grand, so overwhelming! The Christian thinks not. One of the leading Episcopal clergymen of India —one who entertained Joseph Cook when in the East —with whom I was then travelling, was directly asked by me if he sincerely believed that Moses, or any other man, ever actually talked with his Maker here, answered: "It was a rare spiritual experience." It matters not now whether it was more. One view of its sacred peaks is worth the labor of a life-time. Though rent by earthquake and torn by lightning, the influence of this patriarchal mount is ever phenomenal. "And all the people saw the thunderings and the lightnings and the noise of the trumpet, and the mountain smoking; and when the people saw it, they removed afar off."

The captain informed me that the base of Sinai was forty-five miles distant, but when, later, we undertook the journey to the wells of Moses, where only a shallow pool near a few trees remains, despite camel and the undulating plains, it proved a wearisome journey. The wilderness, so-called, is one of sand or brown, arid soil, where nothing but the tamarisk cares to exist, not one of trees and undergrowth. Instead of two peaks, as it appeared from the sea, we found three, each one of which has its claimants as being the true place where Moses received the tablets of the Law —Gebel Mousa, 7359 feet, Gebel Sufsafeh, and Gebel Catherine. A stone chapel and mosque have been built on Mt. Mousa. There are also several caves, as the high, rocky sides are rent in every direction, in one of which Moses may have hidden when the " Lord passed by." The convent of St. Catherine, some 1300 years old in its chapel, at least, is located within 2,360 feet of its summit. A Campanile and Mohammedan mosque stand near. The ascent was so difficult, on account of the intense heat, I did not attempt it. A sheer precipice, 3,000 feet high, of solid rock seamed with porphyry, rose discouragingly on the right, and hot, rough boulders everywhere else, but we could see the Gulf of Akaba, where once rode the fleet of Solomon, glistening in the hot sun, in the east, and our own blue sea, in the course we came, to the west. To see the convent is sufficient. It is so surrounded with a thick and high wall, that the inmates are always safe from theft, robbery, or Bedouins. It has still in existence and in use, the rude windlass for hoisting objects or man to the upper and outer entrance on the walls, once so common in fortified places in the East.

The water is so shallow at Suez, that for four miles one can wade at low tide without danger of drowning, unless the tide, as is said in the case of the Egyptian pursuers of Moses, suddenly returns, when even now you would drown if you could not swim. Suez sits quaintly on a gentle rise out of a vast sandy plain. Between her and the long ridge of sharp hills south is the level plain where Moses divided the waters and passed over dry-shod. The opposite side, up to the wells of Moses, is a barren waste. Some claim the place of crossing a little above, but it does not matter. As you look at Suez, it would seem that one shot from our gun would drive out her entire population, like ants from an ant-hill. The English have a garrison here, as they also have at Alexandria and Cairo. Nothing impresses one in the East, especially in Turkish and Egyptian territory, like the peaceful beauty of the towns and cities. Afar off, they appear raised suddenly out of the ground as by a magician's wand. The dome and minaret are never wanting, and seldom the high whitish wall, and long winding road up to the open gateway. Bathed in the morning or evening sun, they seem ethereal. But not to spoil the pleasant picture we will remain afar off, the farther the better, perhaps, if the view is not lost.

A mile or so out from Suez is Port Ibrahim, from

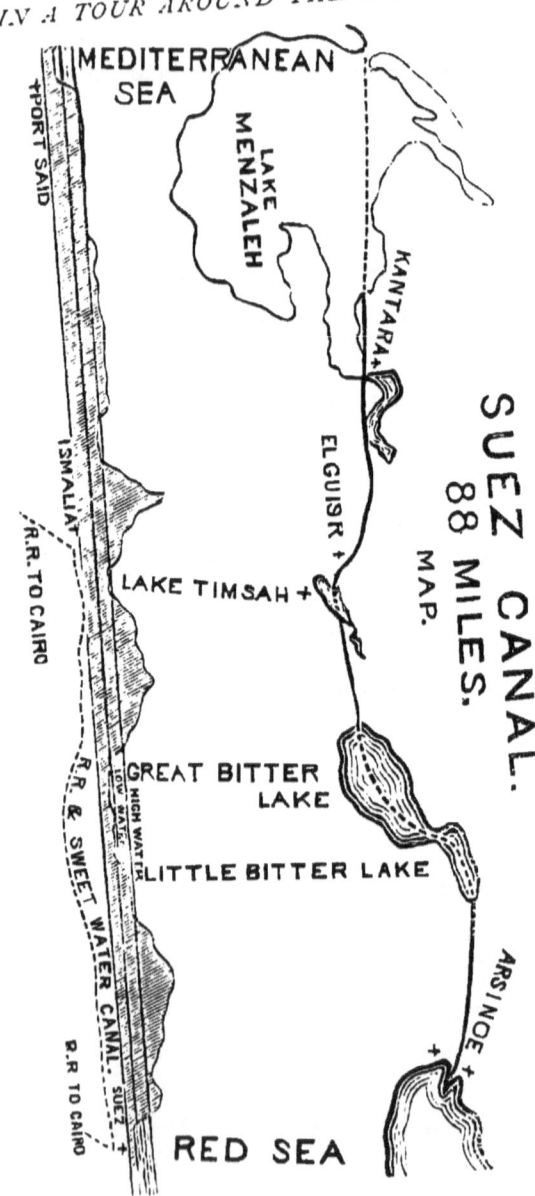

which a train now runs to Cairo. This place is the southern terminus of the celebrated Suez Canal. A few feet south are two lights, one red, the other green. These, upon their firm pedestals, mark its entrance. No steamer is allowed to sail through at night without an electric light high on her forecastle. One Sunday morning, at 8 A. M., we entered here on our way to the Mediterranean. As we advanced, the water rose and fled ahead of us, while that behind rushed headlong after. In places, it seemed hardly possible to insert one's body between the vessel and bank, but, as we slowly glided along, we soon came to a station where the canal opened to sufficient width to admit the passing of an opposite steamer. None but steamers are to be seen. Sailing vessels still round Cape Good Hope. These stations are but turn-outs, and of no great length. Here was ancient Arsinoe or Cleopatris, the old terminus of the ancient canal from Cairo constructed 600 B. C. to carry grain to Mecca. There is now a canal from Suez to the Nile, which supplies the town with fresh water. For centuries, before it was built, they had been obliged to bring it in goatskins from the wells of Moses miles below.

A caravan of camels, on the old trail from Cairo to Mecca, are waiting for us to pass, as we near the first bridge of boats. Two of the boats are soon replaced behind us and, like so many awkward turtles, with head and neck outstretched, they slowly wend their way southward. Nothing but sand, as unbroken as the ocean, lies before and on either side of them. They carry tents, cooking utensils, bedding and food, besides their merchandise. Speaking from experience, journeying by camel is pleasanter when done in the glow of imagination — and by your fireside. If you are of a sensitive nature, you will not feel, after once seeing his ugly head and lips thrust out right before your eyes with a groan too suggestive of the stomach-ache to be borne heroically, much like again mounting his awkward carcass. He does not lie down like the horse or cow. His long hind legs rest on the inner side of his haunches. Even when you are coaxing him to assume that desirable position, so as to save a month or two of precious time trying to crawl up his irregular sides, he so reluctantly complies and with so loud a complaint, that you dread to mount. No sooner mounted, than up pop his hind quarters, just as you have become convinced that it would surely be his fore, and had bent forward accordingly, and lays your tender cheek lovingly — and embrace, too, — upon its long, dirty neck, and you are saved from complete somerset and disgrace, only by a sudden upward jerk of his front. With purple face and bated breath, you may then coax the beast to start. No sooner started, than you repent your imprudence, for the first step once taken, you are set into a backward and forward oscillation about as congenial to your poor frame as an undeserved shaking from a zealous but near-sighted school mistress, in childhood.

But the long line of "ships of the desert" gradually fades away in the distance, so let us return to the canal. Ferdinand Lesseps was not the first to plan this water-way. No less a person than Napoleon Bonaparte had it surveyed years before. And it is a singular fact, that Louis Napoleon, when in exile in America, planned a like one in Nicaragua. The Suez is more properly a water-way than a canal, as it has neither locks, reservoirs, pumping engines, or gates, but in its entire length of eighty-eight miles, its level is barely disturbed, except from the Bitter Lakes to Suez, where there is a slight change, from one to five feet, on account of the tide. Before its construction, the old lakes had fallen to little better than valleys of salty sand, but when the Mediterranean was let in during the winter of 1869, Lakes Menzaleh, Timsah and, later in the following summer, the water from the Red Sea, Little and Great Bitter Lakes became well filled. Sweet water is conducted from the Nile along its entire course. Every five or six miles come the stations or turnouts. These have a signal station, a small cottage surrounded often with date palm and shrubbery, all in the care of the canal servants. The entire route is regulated by telegraph, from Port Said on the north to Suez on the south. Its original cost was $100,000,000 which, of course, must be short of the real sum, from the fact that at one time 30,000 Arabs and Egyptians were forced into service by Mahomet Said Pasha, the Viceroy of Egypt. His successor, Ismail Pasha, refused to comply with the terms of his brother Mahomet. The matter was left out to arbitration, by which the Viceroy was compelled to pay the Canal Company $15,800,000. As the canal was begun in 1860, I think it must have been in 1863 when this trouble arose. It resulted in the permanent withdrawal of conscript labor, and occasioned the use of modern machinery, such as is now being used in the present widening, agreed upon in 1886.

Its depth is intended to be 26 feet, and, when fully widened, the width 72 feet at least. No rock, except a little of soft nature at Ismalia, where there is a slight elevation, was met with the whole distance, the rest being either level sand plain or lake bed. Sixty-six of the eighty-eight miles were excavated, fourteen miles were dredged out, and eight miles needed no labor. By its construction, the distance between India and Western Europe is reduced from 11,379 to 7,628 miles, and when you consider the great number of large vessels and the saving of weeks of valuable time, you begin to realize its vast importance. I think the rate per net ton on each vessel entering this waterway is a little above $1.50. We had obtained at Suez some grapes, apples and cherries. The first were delicious, like the Persian we had in Arabia, but the cherries were like apples, and the apples quite, in flavor and hardness, like our New England quince. Looking over the permit our French commandant had received to pass through, I found it was in English, indicating that England still holds her control. This was corroborated by the English garrison at each end, and the appearance of Englishmen at the numerous turnouts or stations. A telegraph line, on iron and stone posts, runs along the western side, and little marks of iron and stone, numbered, are placed at equal distances on each side. A railway, at some distance on the left, runs to Ismalia, and then turns west and runs down to Cairo. At a short distance up, we came to one of the queer dwellings to be found everywhere in Arabia and Palestine. Its walls, some eight feet high, were built of loose stone. Its roof was of tamarisk branches and roots, and its one opening served both for doorway and window. An aged Arab woman, two bright little urchins and two camels were at home, but we passed on despite the loud invitations to call and share our backsheesh. For a long distance the little boy and girl ran eagerly by our side, begging for food, until some dry bread and vegetables from the cook were cast overboard in their direction, which quickly stopped their clamorous chase.

What these Arabs do for food and drink is a mystery. Those having camels and goats can get along, but how about the camel and goat? On either side, as far as the eye can reach, stretch those plains of dreary sand, three grains of which will change a glass of fresh water quickly into salt. It is evident that some time, if not in the time of Noah, these vast plains were beneath the sea. Even now, at times, the eye catches a glimpse of fields of yellowish-white salt. Now and then, as in Ceylon, fair deposits of kaolin also crop out. We soon came to another bridge of four boats, and another caravan of camels bound for Syria in waiting. An oasis with olive, date, and other trees around a dwelling, could be seen in the distance. Arabs in row-boats were catching a long silvery fish, and others thronged around with plump red dates, too beautiful to look at. At gare-stone 49, 40 or 50 camels with wooden boxes or cars on their backs, were busily engaged in carrying away the banks included in the Cairo side widening. Each Arab had charge of from three to four animals. They were a strange sight, with dark, gloomy faces beneath the universal large white turban, the scant blue cotton dress, and bare legs and feet, actively mingling with the awkward, cloven-footed and long-necked beasts, throwing in the sand on their recumbent bodies, pulling fiercely at their single rein for them to rise, or noisily shouting to get them to back around. Each beast, on arrival, was backed about, like a horse in a cart, and made to kneel. When he went down, he went down as though his legs had suddenly been knocked out from under him, and with such a woe-begone appearance you little expected a rise again even without his heavy load of sand. There they were, constantly falling and rising, at each attempt to rise sticking out their uncouth lips and dismally groaning as in strong protest.

Farther on a similar band was engaged in the same occupation, and still further on mules were operating a little tramway of iron boxes, like those Lesseps is now trying to use on his Panama Canal. To the slow camel, a ride on an empty car drawn by a frisky mule is a great event to the wild Arab. He is yet to learn of the mighty lightning latent therein. "Fwoin baste! fwoin baste!" but as the Irishman was sadly and painfully picking himself up a minute later, he was heard muttering between his set teeth, "Th-a-a ow-l-ld divil!" It will be a revelation to "Pharaoh" when it comes. He will not only marvel at such hidden activity but will quickly let "Israel" go.

After proceeding a little further, we came up with the SS. Pelican, in moorings. We put out hawser fore and aft, and soon were moored also. We were followed by the Telamon, so that three large ocean steamers now lay moored to the left shore. Looking up at the signals, I saw that several balls and pennons were warning us of approaching vessels. As the canal is now and then obstructed by a curve, it is not possible to see but a few hundred feet. The sand dunes here, made by the original excavations, also increased the obstruction. We had now passed both Little and Great Bitter Lakes and the old Cairo canal. After several large steamers had passed, we went on to Lake Timsah, which, though very shallow, is quite large. Here the channel curves around between buoys and lights. Ismalia appears, with green trees, Lesseps's chalet, and several respectable-looking buildings, while a little apart rises the brown and plainly outlined summer residence of the present Khedive. A little steam-launch pays us several short visits, leaving and taking passengers and exchanging pilots. Where we leave the lake, the passage is very narrow and the sides more elevated than elsewhere on the whole canal. I might have taken a train here for Cairo, or caravan for Palestine, but I could not go home without seeing the entire canal, so went on. Here, as on the Nile, were plenty of bull-rushes, but not a single Moses or Pharoah's daughter. Sometimes you see the tamarisk and something like cypress, which are cut and woven into a protection for the banks of the canal, as in some places, as our motion sent the water rushing up the sand, large masses of earth would break off and fall back into the channel. Planks, too, and imported stones are used for the same purpose. About here we saw, on the left, quite a town with a few fine houses and one mosque. It was El Guisr. Boys and girls ran along the banks, begging for backsheesh and food, which they seldom got unless they swam for it, which they often did as eagerly as dogs. The girls wore large earrings and bracelets, which rattled loudly as they walked or ran.

At sunset, upon a distant elevation, peacefully stood a dozen camels beautifully outlined against the golden sky. Only one tall date-palm, with a few Arab tents, seemed to relieve the view. As a picture of simple, joyous and peaceful content, it was an ideal. That night we moored and passed, in the canal. The great desert spread out on either side. Not a bird or beast disturbed the strange solitude. All was as quiet as the grave. The moon and stars came slowly out and turned the sand fields and banks into a mass of glistening gems. To think was as easy as to breathe. The mind seemed inspired, the heart aglow with feeling. Music, dancing, and merry laughter suddenly broke out on the still night, and soon the very banks were covered with groups of merry makers. Round and round, beneath the full, bright moon, whirred rings of joyous people, some in one direction some in another, until off they burst in a wild chase inland. Many of us were content with a quiet walk along the canal, and had a friend not lost a heavy gold bracelet, which obliged our return in search, we might have outwalked the moon. Fortune at last favored us in the finding, but as we were near the boat, we went no farther. The next morning, until 8 o'clock, a thick fog environed us, so we lost several precious hours in inactivity. A few spent the time in fishing, and drew aboard many a pretty little fellow, all gold and silver, like those in the tropics. A man came aboard with a large flock of speckled quail from the wilderness of Sinai. I also saw some cacti growing wild. When under way, the next station had a bright, pretty dwelling, some red flowers and a date-palm. At the next, at stone 24, houses appeared on both sides of the canal, and on the right a garrison of soldiers. There also was a postoffice, from which a small steamer carried and distributed the mail. We now came to Menzaleh Lake or sea, through which the canal was originally laid out as indicated by the dotted lines on the map, but now divided by solid earth-banks thrown up by the dredges. We now passed one of the Anchor Line fast aground, but still had the double passenger-decked Orient, from Australia, just ahead, and three other large steamers behind.

While awaiting downward steamers, another caravan of camels passed. This was the sixth I had seen in less than two days. At this stop four steamers passed, one German, one French, and two English. At station or gare opposite post 7, there were three neat buildings, two date trees, and, away in the distance, another caravan preparing to encamp for the night. Just as the sun was sinking in the west, a loud bugle-call came down upon the quiet air with an effect most startling, followed quickly by a boom of cannon, then still another call. We had reached the Mediterranean.

Right before us, on the left, was a small group of houses and many large docks crowded with shipping. From an Italian man-of-war, or its English neighbor, probably the latter, had come that startling martial sound. There were thirty or more steamers here, and long lines of coal lighters, illuminated by torches, were winding in and out supplying them with coal. Just as we came out, an immense Australian steamship, with its hurricane deck literally packed with men, women, and children, slowly passed. Most of the people were neatly dressed and happily engaged in household and Sunday-school songs. It was an impressive sight. So many leaving home and friends for an untried country, hardship, sickness and possibly death!

This is Port Said, and the Mediterranean, at last. It overlooks the sea, with a high ornamental lighthouse on the right, and a long breakwater, like a huge serpent, running back to the land. I looked behind me. Four immense, dazzling white lights were slowly bearing down from the canal directly upon us, like heavenly bodies broken loose from the sky. They were the electric eye of night, without which no boat in the canal is allowed to advance. We immediately went ashore. Several fair hotels were found, but what I wanted most, a boat for Jaffa, or old Joppa of Paul's time, was wanting. Some Arabs offered to take me over in a sail boat, but, not liking their appearance, I concluded to go on to Alexandria, where my wants would be readily met. So on we went, soon striking into the muddy-colored water of the eastern delta of the Nile. For miles you can look out before you and see its irregular line of demarkation from the pretty blue of the rest of the Mediterranean. A fresh breeze started up and drove away the many flies that had hovered about the vessel in the canal. Early the next morning, we again fell in with a broad expanse of yellowish-green water, which told me that we were opposite the western mouth of the Nile. Plenty of native sail-boats, but only one steamer, dotted the water.

Soon after passing the yellowish sea border, Alexandria came gradually into view. High land, with forts and palaces, was backed by a large dome to the south. Large breaks in the walls appeared in every direction, showing that the late English bombardment had been no mere child's play. The Khedive's palace, with its plain, smooth walls and quaint Moorish architecture, soon disclosed itself behind a breakwater and lighthouse, then a dismantled fort on the west of the channel which leads up to the inner harbor and docks. A pretty Mohammedan mosque, in an unfinished state, lies a little farther to the west. I was told it had lain in that condition for some time, and it would never be completed, as it was their custom to stop all work on an edifice of religious nature on the death of the Khedive who begins the work. I take another look at the Kedive's palace, for there it was that Arabi and his followers demanded the abdication of their ruler, and attempted his assassination. An English garrison stands close at hand, and many a trace of shot and shell are still observed in the neighborhood. Pompey's Pillar, away up on an elevation in the distance, caught my eye before I had hardly thought of its present existence. As soon as we ceased to move, the same pell-mell rush, as in the East, but more annoying, after our freight and passengers again began. It was a tug-of-war. Arabs, Turks, Greeks, Montenegrins, and what not, pulled, pushed, and made boisterous capture. Did I know Admiral Franklin?—this swarthy fellow was once in the United States Navy—and other less gentle reminders that he was the guide for me, and if one were humored, a dozen crowded around and menaced him to leave, and so on. If there were ever a Babel, surely Alexandria is one. I shook them all off; would have tumbled the whole lot overboard if I had possessed the strength; and went on shore with the officers of the Volga, on the company's steam-launch.

Those who caught hold of my companions were promptly and soundly kicked, for as we went down the outside gangway, the natives caught hold of our clothing and tried to drag us into their boats. It was a good lesson, for it made me keep on my guard everywhere I went in this strange land. The French are loud and earnest in their condemnation of the English in their policy in Egypt, and regard the latter as having no higher motive than to squeeze the country dry and then throw it rudely away. As I was having my baggage examined, it was suggested more than once, that a fee to the official would save delay and trouble, and to my surprise, I often saw it done. For myself, however, it seemed so dishonest, I always refused. The streets, from the docks up to the square, have sidewalks, but through the market which I visited to view the native grains and fruit, the middle of the street was thronged with merchants, dealers, buyers and passers-by. Graceful and noble looking women with veiled faces, a queer ring and bar lattice over their shapely noses, and long ear-rings, wide bracelets, anklets, and long rows of convex silver disks strung across the forehead, merrily jingling in the air, erect as queens, crowd you on every side with urns, vases and receptacles of every kind and material on the head or in the hand.

By chance you catch a glimpse of large, solemn black eyes beneath the veil which feminine curiosity or a chance breeze has brushed aside. Of course you here can gaze at a woman straight in the eye, if you wish. You get about as much pleasure by so doing as in staring at an empty negro mask at home. The men and boys are dressed in all styles imaginable, but usually in a way approaching their different native costumes. Both in Cairo and Alexandria besides Arabs,

Greeks and Montenegrins, there are many French, Germans and Italians.

AN EGYPTIAN WOMAN AND CHILD.

I found the square, where the European families stood siege and were so cruelly butchered, rebuilding on a grander scale than ever before. A large equestrian statue of one of their heroes ornaments the easterly section. A funeral, with all on foot and an immense catafalque covered and borne by men, passed before me as I entered. One of the queerest and most laughable sights are the little donkeys trotting along the streets, belabored from behind by shouting donkey boys or drivers. The poor animal, pegging along with two hundred pounds of European beef-eater on its weak back, reminds one of a toad under a harrow. Alexandria was for years the capital of Egypt, and from the fourth century before Christ to the seventh century after, it was the seat of literature and learning in the whole East. The famous Pharos, planned by Dinocrates, who rebuilt the temple of Diana at Ephesus, stood 400 feet high, not far northeast of Fort Ada, the Harem and the Palace.

After Ptolemy Alexander gave the city to the Romans, it was regarded the chief city in the world next to Rome. On its capture by Omar, every effort was made to save its large and valuable library, then the largest in the world, but in vain. "If the books contain the same doctrine as the Koran, they are unnecsssary, and if contrary doctrines, they surely must be destroyed," said that worthy. So books, requiring years of study and self-sacrificing toil, were distributed about the city and used for fuel. Pompey's Pillar, a single shaft of red granite, 73 feet long, and 29 feet 8 inches around, rises from a mound in the old part of the city 40 feet high. It has a capital in the Corinthian style 9 feet high, and a base, making its net height about 99 feet. It was once surmounted by a statue of the Roman Emperor Diocletian, and its tablet informs you that the whole was erected in his honor. The city, before the opening of the Suez Canal, was of great importance, from the fact that the Eastern and Australian steamers ran up the Red Sea to Suez, and there landed passengers, mail and freight to be transported hither by rail for shipment; but now only a very few passengers come that way, and no foreign freight.

The catacombs, hewn out of soft rock, are located in the old part near the mosque, and some large stone wind-mills, unseen outside of Holland. Near by is an elevation with a grove of date-palms. The latter were so tempting I could not help lingering, long gazing up the slim trunks rising sixty feet into the sky, and admiring the long clusters of rich, red dates heavily drooping downward. The pendant fruit, in general appearance, looks like an immense barberry cluster, although the depth and shade of color is quite unlike. In Arabia I had plucked the fruit when turning from yellowish-green to this ripe red, and held them up to the sun. The sweet juices were plainly seen grouping and crystalizing into sugar. This experiment was generally quickly followed by a sudden movement mouthward, and all was soon over. Ah, how I miss those gurgling juices! For the first time in all my long journey, I found the Bank of England note at 3 per cent discount, and English and American gold nearly the same. The brokers here sit out on the street before a low cabinet, in which they keep their queer collections of money, and transact business as though it were but a peanut stand. Of the coin, I can only remember the mejideh, a large silver coin of the size of our dollar, the piastre, silver like our dime, para, and a lot of other copper coins from the size of our dollar down to the old half-cent.

Having viewed the town, we went down to the southwest end for the train, and I was soon bowling along up the Nile to Cairo, about five hours' ride, or 150 miles by rail. We were, at first, impressed with the similarity between this city and Alexandria. Mounds of rubbish disfigure its otherwise picturesque exterior. A massive citadel in the southern part stands in place of the great dome in the centre of new Alexandria, and the narrow, crooked streets and mud houses of both cities are identical; but, on the whole, I liked both this city and its mixed or varied population much better. It has several wide streets, and the one over which we drove to the pyramids was well shaded by acacia and sycamore trees. An iron bridge here spans the Nile, and if one has no desire to go into the suburbs beyond Bulak, he can now do so with a little comfort and pleasure. A large part of the capital has of late been improved, so that it looks as well as any European city. The English have garrisons, a permanent colony and a church, and the Germans have all but the garrison, but the Mohammedans outnumber all other people and religious sects two to one, and have about 400 mosques, which add a picturesque effect to the whole city that would be impossible to obtain in any other way.

The citadel rises 250 feet above the streets, and is said to have been built by Saladin in 1166. This contains a mosque of Oriental alabaster, and a palace built by Mahomet Ali. In this section of the city rises its most beautiful edifice, the Mosque of Sultan Hasan. It was built in 1357, and bewilders the eye with the grandeur of its arches and cornices, its minerets, domes and delicate tracery. Words fail to represent Oriental splendor. Many a time I have stood gazing, with full consciousness that my eyes might never in this life view such scenes again, while from the arched doorways the stalwart Turk, in pure white turban, gold-lace jacket and flowing dress, gravely paced the neighboring tessellated pavement. The grand, the magnificent and the delicate, all are here. It but wants the slanting rays of the setting sun to reproduce St. John's ideal of Heaven. Many such a sight, and perhaps in these identical places, he may have seen and treasured up, to appear again, as in his lonely prison he penned the Revelation. Bulak, a suburb on the northwest, contains, besides a hospital, a cotton mill, a paper mill, a Government printing-press and a museum of Egyptian antiquities. The latter of which should certainly be visited.

Up the Nile a short drive, on the island opposite old Cairo, stands a pillar some forty feet high, inserted in a well-shaped inclosure fifteen feet wide. It is the Nilometer or means of determining the height of the river's annual rise. The water always rises to thirty-two feet, but forty feet is the most desirable point, as a less rise would not fertilize so large an extent of country as desirable, while to rise above that point would mean injury, if not destruction, to both country and property. The Nile had now reached its height, and was beginning to subside. Over opposite was a palace and harem. A little to the north is where Moses was found playing with the frogs and bulrushes. A few hours before, I had been shown where, as they claim, the Ark rested, also the spot where my noted namesake was so obedient that the Lord sent an animal to butt against some neighboring trees to draw away his old father's attention. If the truth were told, I believe Abraham was first made aware of its presence by sudden activity in the rear, and that it was no less than a determination to get even with the little rascal that led at last to Isaac's fortunate escape.

From here it is but six miles to the pyramids, and along a road shaded somewhat by trees. Palms are seen, and also fir trees, on our left, the blue Nile stretching out before, and a little to one side the lofty triangles piercing the sky. They seem nearly as high here at Cairo as on the journey, and when you have paid your mejideh to the neighboring sheik, and stand at the base, there still is little change except in the greater roughness of the exterior or the protuberance of their side-layers. The first you visit is that of Cheops, 780 feet high, with a base of 764x764 feet. It is said that it employed 360,000 men for twenty years to complete it, and 100,000 men ten years to construct a suitable way from the Nile over which to transport the immense granite blocks, which had been brought by water from the quarries hundreds of miles above. It seems plain that the idea that the body would again be tenanted by the soul led to these stupendous tombs. There are three large and three small pyramids here. The summit of the Cheops is 32 feet square. The entrance is always from the North, uneven, circuitous and on many levels. Sarcophagi have been found in all, and mummies of many of the early Egyptian rulers now rest in the Bulak, French and British Museums. The Sphinx, a lion's body with human head, stands but a short distance away, a giant in form but shorn of much of its beauty and attractiveness. It seems to be cut from the solid rock. Its true height is supposed to be 142 feet. It is said to be 102 feet around its forehead. Beneath its enormous nostrils

THE PYRAMIDS FROM ACROSS THE NILE.

was stationed an altar for sacrifice, as it was a local deity. Memphis, the ancient capital of Egypt, lies a little farther on to the southeast of the Sphinx. Only a few hillocks remain to identify its site.

But I have detained you too long, so let us return by beautiful Rhodes, the whirling dervishes or priests, to the spot where the ruler used to ride horseback over the prostrate forms of the returned Mecca pilgrims. Far from the southeast section, even now, as of old, large caravans go out on this still sacred pilgrimage, although they seldom now exceed 7,000 against 25,000, as formerly. They leave and return annually, and both occasions are sacredly observed as holidays. By arched doorways, through which I can see fountains playing and orange blossoms, through narrow, covered streets to the canal, and then to the station, I reach the railway and return to the Mediterranean. As I leave the dock to walk aboard the steamer, a group of veiled women are sifting scattered grain and coffee, to free it from the gravel and dirt for home use, a sight not uncommon in any Eastern city where economy is imperative.

The women of Northern Egypt wear a more elaborate costume than I had seen for months. It may be on account of European influence. The men wear flowing trousers, a small vest, an embroidered jacket and low cap, or large white turban. The women, besides the first-mentioned article, have dress open at the sides, gold lace jacket with long, flowing sleeves, a white muslin veil from their forehead running back, and a similar one flowing down over their face so as to protect all but the eyes, and often reaching as low as the hem of their dress. In strong contrast to their soft, clear, dark complexions stand out the strings of white ornaments festooned from brow or clasped about their shapely necks and shoulders. When you meet one such like Miriam in the wilderness giving expression to her pent-up joy, you see poetry of motion in lines you never forget. Another common scene is that with the skilful but sly necromancer. He is everywhere. The first I met was a strapping great fellow, in huge white turban, green jacket, and trousers so full as to resemble a skirt. In a wide cotton girdle he carried several ancient coins, a knife, some matches, two scorpions, and one of the loveliest white and yellow rabbits ever seen. The number and nature of his strange performances were startling. He would put one of his coins into your hand and request you to hold it firmly. Then, with an upward glance, murmuring "Allah! Allah!" he would make outward passes with his arms and suddenly stop, bend down and pick out the very coin from between the ugly scorpion's feet. It is the first intimation of his trick, and before opening your hand you instinctively press your fingers more closely to make sure the coin is still there. To your bewildering astonishment you feel little but your own soft palm. You nervously open it. You find just what you felt — absolutely nothing.

He next takes the two squirming scorpions and, as though they were so many rich dates, slowly chews them up. He then commences to playfully tease the gentle little rabbit, which stands up, rolls over, curls up its pretty feet and goes to sleep on its woolly back until, with a strange, hollow murmur, this man's two fingers are inserted into the little fellow's mouth, which now, we remember, had been growing fuller and fuller, until its cheeks stood out like those of Jacky Horner, and drawn slowly forth is one wriggling, yellowish scorpion, closely followed by the other. He next unwound from his head his long white turban, twelve or more feet in length, and doubled it. Giving one end to one of us, he drew his knife and deliberately severed it in the middle. We all, at his request, examined the separated parts, and promptly returned them to the owner. He stooped and struck a match. Rising, he held the lighted match beneath the severed ends until they flamed and became charred. Then, taking the charred ends and gently blowing out the flames, he carefully rubbed the injured fabric between his palms, muttering in soft, liquid tones, "Allah! Allah! Allah!" when, with a slow, graceful flourish, he sent floating out in the air before our very faces the same length of spotless white, the old turban reunited, and while we looked to one another in amazement, he silently aproached, and in a most insinuating way implored "Backsheesh! backsheesh!"

But the time had come to bid Egypt adieu.

It was a lovely night, with the stars like moons in their effulgence, and the moon like a burnished silver shield. The dancing waves, tipped with silver, ran merrily before a stiff breeze and lapped the vessel's side with soft, pleasant sounds, as if in tender caress. Our swarthy pilot, in red and gold, disappeared at last over the rail, his large, white turban reflecting light not very unlike the moon above, and was soon wafted back to harbor, and we were left to pursue our course alone. It was a fitting occasion for contemplation, and yet thought failed to come. Even now, Egypt holds me speechless. China seems like a babe compared with this ancient home of man. The more you see, the more irresistible its influence. Even the bulrush and papyrus are as potent as its rivers and the pyramids. Like the annual rise and fall of its sacred Nile, nations have risen to power only to disappear again, and we almost feel like pitying Arabi in his deplorable failure to succeed in the unification and improvement of his people. Arabi was brave, but of no great knowledge even of his native land. As I saw him strolling along the shore in his exile home in Colombo, I did not realize the great need of a new prophet to his native people, or the tender attachment he must have felt for Cairo, where he lived and was captured. Perhaps, he determined, if taken at all, to surrender in this his Heaven. As he paces the silent shore at sunset, and gazes on the western sky, his imagination can easily picture the splendor and magnificence of his home beneath.

A COIN FROM CAIRO.

CHAPTER VIII.

*The jackal in the field,
The Turk within the town,
Alas, fair Holy Land!*

FROM Alexandria to Jaffa it is a good fifteen hours' sail, and then you have to take your chance of landing safely, or, at least, getting a good ducking. The Arab boats cluster around, as soon as your arrival becomes known, and thus you fortunately escape being carried beyond to Beyrout. As you catch a first glimpse of its terraced slopes and low buildings, you are a little disappointed, as it fails to please one just hailing from the splendor of Cairo. Yet this is the oldest harbor in the world. The King of Tyre brought here the cedars of Lebanon for Solomon's temple, and, if tradition is correct, it was here that Noah built the Ark. Jonah is also said to have sailed from here, and judging from the boisterous sea, it is most likely that Jonah was here cast up. It is no miracle. Ask my suffering companions. They still show you the house of Simon, the tanner, where Peter had his vision, and recalled Tabitha to life. Although on a hillside, and with poor and dirty streets, it has some pretty orange and lemon trees, and also the tall cypress, for partial compensation. Jaffa at one time stood seige from Napoleon, but was obliged at last to yield. You leave for Jerusalem as soon as you can get conveyance, and if early in the morning, you can reach it the same night, and also see Lydda, its Church of St. George destroyed by Saladin, and still an interesting ruin, and Ramleh with its three convents and two mosques. This place was the scene of many encounters between Saladin and the Crusaders under Richard Cœur de Lion. It is but a small town.

You next come to Emmaus, where the Lord met his two disciples, whose hearts burned but knew him not, for it was after his crucifixion. As you catch a glimpse of the Holy City in the distance, with its solid, high wall, its many domes and minarets, you are quickly carried back to Egypt, and if one would be content to remain outside and ride around to the north and east, his pleasure would quite appease his high anticipations. But the moment you enter the Jaffa gate, you know what to expect, and if you do not, you soon find it. Were it not for seeing the Mosque of Omar and the Church of the Holy Sepulchre, I should beg you not to enter, that you might think of this once proud city as one of purity and light. The Turk is everywhere—soldier, magistrate and police. The money is Turkish, the dress is Turkish, the smell is Turkish. There appears to be nothing, unless you dig down thirty or forty feet beneath all this rubbish and filth, to which the Christian can pin his faith. Would you bathe in the pool of Siloam? Only in imagination, friend. 'Tis very bad. Would you sit by sweet, gliding Kedron and list to its gentle murmur? After you have succeeded in trying a hundred or two of the hot stones in its dry bed, each one hotter than the other, and wasted nearly a year of your life waiting for a sight of water, you will sadly repent and suddenly move on. You will then, perhaps, mournfully appreciate the western wail and lift up your voice with the many unhappy Jews there assembled, and refuse to be comforted. This is the Jews' "Wailing Place," where the stones are worn smooth by their lips. Every Friday they here crowd around and loudly lament over the loss of their Holy City.

The Church of the Holy Sepulchre, among other

things, includes within its sacred walls the stone where the Lord's body was anointed before burial, the stone where the Angel sat announcing the Resurrection, the tomb itself, six feet square, containing a white marble sarcophagus, where the body of Christ lay, and where Mary saw the two angels, where forty-two gold and silver lamps, presented by different European rulers are kept constantly burning, the square platform of Calvary where Christ was crucified—though the place is probably outside the Damascus gate—and many other objects of real interest, even if not believed authentic.

By passing south through the Jaffa gate, you will in six hours be able to see Bethlehem a little to the south, and get a sight of Hebron farther on. A short distance out is the Elias Convent, where that prophet was fed by the angels. Bethlehem is a pretty and attractive town seen at a distance, and, strange to say, nearly all of its inhabitants are Christians. Here, in a monastery, is shown the place of the Nativity. It is within a church of Lebanon cedar, built in the fourth century by Helena, mother of Constantine, and is the oldest Christian church in the world. You descend a flight of steps, and enter a marble hall, 38x12 feet. A silver star at the eastern end attracts your immediate attention. You read:

"HIC DE VIRGINE MARIA JESUS CHRISTUS NATUS EST."

In a recess is a marble manger. Here, then, is a marble manger in a cave. If you step into the Church Santa Maria Maggiore in Rome, you will find a wooden manger, claimed to be the genuine original. St. Jerome lived and died here, in a neighboring grotto, and not far beyond is a chapel where the angel herald sang:

"PEACE ON EARTH, GOOD WILL TO MEN."

Hebron lies still farther south, and in its precincts lies the cave of Macpelah, with the bones of Abraham and Sarah, Isaac and Rebecca, and Leah and Joseph. The spot is marked by a mosque.

Jericho, the Jordan, and the Dead Sea require about two days, and is an interesting trip. Leaving the eastern gate you descend into a valley and ascend the Mount of Olives, over the road Christ often passed on his way to Bethany, and if you take the road to the right you will soon see Bethany right before you. Poor, dilapidated Bethany! You are constantly descending until you reach New Jericho. It is a mere mass of loose stone huts, like those in Arabia, and of very forbidding appearance. When you reach the placid lake sparkling between the high banks below, you are by the Dead Sea, 1300 feet below the Mediterranean, with Jerusalem 4000 feet above you. Rushes, reeds and overhanging trees enclose its northern border, and nothing unusually unpleasant detracts from its quiet beauty. It is salt, heavy and buoyant, however, as one would expect, and were it not for the constant accession of the fresh water of the Jordan, it would be much more so. The Jordan is soon reached, and can be crossed by either ford or bridge. It is a memorable stream, and yet you fail to realize how it formerly looked. Now, at the ford, the steep fall to the Dead Sea gives it a strong current. Formerly the willows and rushes can hardly have been so abundant. It was then probably more than fifty feet wide.

As you pass over the level plain, where once old Jericho stood, memory recalls its former splendor of palm and fruit gardens. Near here, Herod the Great lived and died. These groves and gardens Cleopatra received as a gift from Mark Antony. Here occurred the clever scene of

"Zaccheus he did climb the tree,
His Lord to see."

As illustrated in the old New England Primer. His house is pointed out occupied by a Turkish guard, but it is strange they do not show a like ingenuity in exhibiting the tree. Armenians, Syrians, Greeks, Copts, Russians, English, French and Americans all flock down through this plain to view where Elijah led Elisha through Jordan's waters, and ascended to Heaven. Where Christ was baptized by John, where Joshua and the Israelites crossed, where Namaan was healed of leprosy, and Elisha made an axe-head float. If the said instrument had a wooden head — or the reporter of the event, which is more likely — it is quite explicable. Sodom and Gomorrah are supposed to have been located near the Dead Sea just below. Where on its high banks no one knows. The only points about the sea, of interest to me, were its great depth of 1,300 feet, and its surprising gravity and buoyancy. The axe, if broad, like the ancient battle axe, might here even now for a considerable time remain suspended on its surface.

It was farther towards the Jordan that I met the only attractive flower in all this wild region. It was a magnificent oleander. This flower seems never to miss the care of man, and grows wild by the banks of the river, a proud survivor of the country's former glory. As far as I could observe, it is the Germans alone who have restored any great part of Judea to its former condition or fruitfulness. They have settled here and there, founded schools and churches, and tilled the soil till it blossoms like the rose. Away from this people, nothing but spiritual experiences out of the country's associations with Bible history can make your journey even tolerable. Your property, person, life, even, is as unsafe beyond the Eastern gate of Jerusalem as in the Middle Ages. A party of Americans were surrounded and captured by Bedouins to the south of me, and a party of Englishmen just a little to the north, and although I escaped a like experience, it was by the skin of my teeth. My enforced stay, also, at a place where the livelong night, a grizzy old Arab, at regular intervals, broke out in fierce complaint, in a tone calculated to awaken both Abraham and Ishmael, was nearly as bad, for repeated fright is often worse than death. The dress of the people varies according to the nationality. The Turk, as in Egypt, has low cap or large turban, broad trousers, and red or yellow morocco shoes; the Arab, cap or turban, flowing dress and bright sash. Besides these there are many Copts, Jews and Armenians. The latter are generally Christians, and are constantly leaving their native land to escape the tyranny of the Shah of Persia, who is Mohammedan. Several young men, who had evaded the Shah's commands that no Armenian should leave the country, came to Europe in my company, and one to New York. Their aim is education for the ministry, so they can return and better cope with the Mohammedan. What I saw of Mohammedanism in its mosques, a standing crowd beneath the reader's desk, now in response and now in loud lamentations, awakened too mixed a feeling to appreciate their form of worship. The splendor of the edifice seemed profaned. Perhaps it is but a type of our own spiritual life in the "Temple not made by hands."

Many scenes familiar to the Bible student are daily encountered. The ox, threshing or drawing the rude one-handled wooden plough, the tare and the wheat, the lily of the field, the goatskin water bottles swung over the shoulder, the sandal, the fig and palm trees, the hand mill for grinding grain, and the ass, raven and vulture. One more I must add, the most potent and sacred, around which often memory clings as on no other object. As we return from the Jordan and pass over the brow of Mt. Olivet, we descend towards a valley and stop by an enclosure containing some half a dozen ancient trees. Gnarled, seared and broken, they awaken a feeling of pity for themselves alone, but feeling deepens when we recognize that this lonely spot is Gethsemane, the garden of our Savior's grief. We linger long and tenderly, assured, at last, its past was real indeed. This we could feel, this no man change, and slowly to the gate, turning now and then for yet one more last look, we passed into the busy crowd.

The next day I was again bounding along the deep, blue sea in the same course taken by Paul to prosecute his appeal to Cæsar. Cyprus, Crete and Clauda in turn passed before my view, and strange to say, the vessel of each was from Alexandria. Greece from a low coast begins at Navarino to grow bolder, till soon nothing but mountains and ravines appear. Zante, a good-sized island with hilly interior and sloping sides, soon appeared in view. It is dotted over with scattering dwellings, and much of its soil is given up to the cultivation of a small, seedless grape, which is dried and exported under the name of currant. Contrary to general belief, it is not a bush fruit like our currant, nor is its culture confined to this pretty island. In western Greece I found the same fruit in large quantities. The slopes were bright with grain, and fig and olive trees. Zante is its leading place on the east coast. Next followed the large island Cephalonia, with its pretty seaport, Argostoli. Missolonghi, where Byron fought and died, lies just across the deep, blue water in the rear. Next came Corfu, with its pretty and attractive hills. As far as you can see to the right, the Gulf of Patras stretches out towards Corinth and eastern Greece. To the south, the Gulf of Arcadia, with Olympia, celebrated for the ancient Grecian games, looms up in the distance. Farther back, away to the east, lie Mts. Parnassus and Olympus.

While conversing with the captain, he informed me of his early life, and pointed out to me his native town nestling among the hills of Cephalonia. Night or day, in this fresh, healthy climate, one loves to breathe. Beneath you lies the deep-blue, white-fringed wave, and above, in the wide expanse of sapphire sky, no cloud by day and myriads of flashing, brilliant lights swinging ever nearer to your side at night. Four of my companions were young Brahmins from the interior of India on their way to England for a collegiate course at Oxford. Until they left their native land, they had never seen the sea, and their handsome, manly faces always lighted up in enthusiastic contemplation of nature's brilliant panorama. Passing thus along the bold coast of Turkey and Montenegro, we soon made a western tack and saw the old castle of Fred. II. and Charles XII. rising out of the sea directly before us. This, then, is Brindisi, Diomed's town, where ended the old Appian way mentioned by Horace and Roman historians. Here Irene wedded Roger, son of Tancred, and here, also, Virgil died. Here came the noble Roman to embark for Greece, and the Crusader for the land of Saladin. It is now the port for the Australian and India English mail route, and lies at the extreme south-eastern point of Italy. We were soon alongside of a dock with two modern hotels just across the street, and old Roman ruins on either side. Away over across the bay rose two pretty villas occupied by Italian wine merchants. The olive, fig, pomegranate and grape, in the rich soil and mellow air, are fast ripening. Drawn by one shaft horse, with a donkey or smaller horse tugging at its side, dyed purple with wine, and slopping the rich juice like water, are constantly rolling by large, long barrel-like wagons of wine fresh from the vintage.

A little farther on another liquid is being transported in a more primitive and laughable fashion. A large goat is calmly leading a full half dozen or more companions along the open street, tinkling a large cow-bell suspended from her neck, while behind lazily trudge a man and boy calling out the well-known milkman's cry.

A woman issues forth from a neighboring doorway and holds out a jar, whereupon, after some searching, the old man finds the desirable source of supply and, sinking down, abstracts just the quantity of lacteal fluid ordered, and deliberately turns it into the customer's receptacle. Years ago, I saw the same experiment near Hyde Park, London, but on that time, with the nobler animal, the cow. While entering the park, I saw a sign, on one of the booths, advertising the sale of fresh milk, and turning, I saw a girl approach the gentle animal and extract about a pint of fresh, rich liquid, and hand it to her waiting customer, who publicly swallowed it as greedily as a young calf.

Walking up into the place, I found two very old cathedrals, one not much in use, towards which a long line of men, women and children were swiftly moving. Behind the leader, bearing his full hands aloft, came stout priests, a bier with remains, and a group of black dressed women tearing their hair, throwing up their arms wildly into the air, and filling the ear with piercing lamentations. Not far distant stood forty or fifty men in pairs. As they moved, I heard the jingle of steel, and approaching, I observed that each couple was united by a chain, and that all were, in turn, fastened to a longer chain between them. A small guard of Italian soldiers seemed to have them in charge. They were prison convicts, interrupted in their course to the water by the long funeral procession to the Cathedral.

Women and girls sit at their doorways winding off from reels cotton and linen thread and yarn, while within could be heard the well-known sound of shuttle and reed. High on a terrace, overlooking the pretty land-locked harbor and its sea castle beyond, are two weather-beaten columns, one a symbol of Italy's rare fertility of soil for vine culture, and the other commemorating in old Latin, too defaced to be legible, some important local event.

But little can be seen of the old road to Rome, described so vividly by Horace. For centuries this was the main thoroughfare to Greece, and many a philosopher, statesman and poet has trod the way my feet were then taking. The way is there, but a large part of the town was destroyed by an earthquake in 1416. As if there were to be an instant repetition of that calamity, the church bells suddenly burst out in wild jargon. What a noise for such a little place! It brought back my former experiences in the North of Italy where, years ago, it seemed to me that every house contained a bell, and every street a priest. After seeing the town it became necessary for me to choose whether I would continue on with my Palestine companions, or continue with my original plan. As I never had sailed the blue Adriatic, or seen much of Turkey and Austria, I concluded to separate and go to Trieste and Venice. When about to set sail, my attention was drawn to a crowd around a returning fisherman, who was actively jumping around and trying to run a knife into a queer-looking object in the bottom of his boat. It was not a fish, neither did it look much like a crab, yet numerous long tentacles, like so many serpents, opened and closed as if to crush everything within reach. I had seen the same creature before, so it was not long before I made it plain to an army friend that it was an octopus. On the shores of the Eastern Islands they often are a terror, and feared more than the shark, for once in the grasp of one of these strong creatures, it is almost impossible to wound them so that they will release their hold, and they are soon scrambling off with their prey. Passing two large laurel wreaths hung in memory of Victor Emmanuel, we saluted the guard and went on board.

Out towards the bold, rough country of Montenegro, and hugging the rough Turkey shore, we soon bowled along the blue Adriatic as in a dream. Fleecy clouds, driven by the breeze, kept us jolly company, while just above, others were skurrying as fast in the opposite direction. Often on the ocean, in the trade winds, this phenomenon is more marked, for besides the lower stratum of clouds accompanying the vessel and the next upper as swiftly flying in the opposite direction, there is still a higher, either stationery or apparently following the vessel's course. Herzegovina and Dalmatia were soon seen and passed. A very few villages in these wild countries are so open to view as to be plainly seen. As soon as we reached Austria the rain fell in torrents, and drove me to the piano for occupation.

It not long after cleared away, however, as suddenly as it came, and right before my startled eyes, as if growing out of the rippling sea, rose green foliage, massive edifices and mighty domes. It was a scene of real enchantment. Instead of the high and rugged hills of a few hours before, solid masonry with nothing but the water, apparently, to spring from soon stood out on both sides of me, as firmly as if carved from solid rock. We were crossing the Grand Canal of Venice. St. Maria della Salute, with its immense dome and grand proportions, was in plain view until I reached the dock. Boats, long, slender and low, propelled by one oar in the hands of a standing oarsman, flocked to the vessel's side, and we were soon seated in the little queer cabin of a gondola. These long, narrow boats are in deep black, and many of their cabins, which arise like a buggy top in the centre, are richly carved. They run to a sharp line each end, and carry a little torch for night use. They serve the place of our hacks, coaches and horse-cars, as the streets of Venice are water-ways only. A small steam-launch, now, also plies up the Grand Canal, the principal street, so to speak. But, if you have the courage, you can find narrow walks alongside of the houses, over tiny arched bridges and through its small squares.

I soon became so familiar with these in my trips after the Rialto, Bridge of Sighs, and St. Mark's, that, to-day, I feel perfectly safe in any part of this quaint old city. The place is built on seventy-two islands and is rightly called the "Queen of the Adriatic." Its 146 water-ways are crossed by 306 stone bridges, each like the Rialto, which is located some distance up the Grand Canal, steeply rising and laid with steps.

The Rialto differs, however, in having two walls separating the middle way, or bazaar, from the crossings on each side. Its stone steps are worn into deep hollows, though the amount of business transacted in the queer place cannot be very great. Shakespeare has immortalized the place, however, and the American tourist should leave the gondola and climb its rough steps once, at least, or he will afterwards regret it. The old Bridge of Sighs has a sadder interest.

> "My beautiful, my own,
> My only Venice — this is breath! Thy breeze,
> Thine Adrian sea breeze, how it fans my face!
> The very winds feel native to my veins,
> And cool them into calmness!"

It had quite escaped my mind, when turning to the left from the avenue leading from St. Mark's to the water, my eye happened to glance up and rested, in an instant, upon a covered way from the Doge's Palace to the massive granite prison, even now with iron-barred windows. Byron has truthfully written, —

> "I stood in Venice, on the Bridge of Sighs;
>   A palace and a prison on each hand;
>   I saw from out the waves her structures rise,
>   As from the stroke of the enchanter's wand."

It is high in the air, above the second story, at least, and beneath flows a narrow, sluggish canal into the sea. In the right hand building were confined state and other prisoners. It is a gloomy though substantial building even now. Over this high-covered way was led in chains the poor unfortunate to receive his sentence in the building opposite. This edifice was a palace, grand even now but showing signs of decay, and in process of substantial repair on its water side.

But let me not forget St. Mark's Cathedral. It must have been nearly 2 P. M. when I entered a large arched passageway of the Royal Palace, and found myself face to face with a long, narrow, paved square. Hundreds of eager doves, like snow-flakes, filled the air and so obstructed the view that for some minutes nothing else could be distinguished. When finally settled, the pavement seemed literally covered with them. I now saw before me, rising to a great height, a square, reddish tower, which I recognized as the Campanile, or bell tower. At its base stood a lady and attendant, who but a few minutes before, I suppose, had strewn the square with grain. Not knowing the hour for this well-known and pretty custom, it took me quite by surprise, but nothing could exceed my joy when my eyes caught sight, a little to the left of the bell tower, of the sweeping arches, gilded tracery, and soft colors of St. Mark's. Surely, it was a vision! If it is so beautiful to-day, what must have been its effect when fresh and new! It dates back to 829, when it was founded as a ducal chapel, but did not become a cathedral until 1807. Its architects were from Constantinople, who imported 600 marble pillars to support its massive decorations, from distant Greece. Grandly rises before you one mighty arch or alcove, richly adorned with bright, colored mosaics and gold. This is flanked on each side with others of smaller radius, but alike radiant with decorations, blending the Moorish so happily with the Italian style that you are quite content in thinking yourself in both Cairo and Rome at the same time. The bronze horses of Chio, brought as plunder from Constantinople in 1206, and in turn taken by Napoleon, in 1797, to adorn the triumphal arch in the Place du Carrousel in Paris, now replaced stand conspicuously forth from marble arch and column.

The spot where, in 1177, Frederick Barbarossa and Pope Alexander III. met in reconciliation is marked by a small, reddish tile in the vestibule. The pavement is worn and cracked, but is richly built of agate, jasper and colored marble. The columns are of porphyry and verd-antique, while both inside and out large and rich pictures in mosaic greet the eye in every direction. A piece of the Saviour's dress, the stone on which he stood while preaching to the people of Tyre, and many other precious relics are still shown you here. The whole square is surrounded by princely buildings, flanked on the outer side by tessellated, arched walks or passageways, among which are the Doges Palace, the Palace of the Nobles, and Royal Palace. Near by is the Library of St. Mark, containing many rare manuscripts, such as Homer's Iliad and a part of the Odyssey, of Sophocles, and nearly all the works of Cicero. Nearly opposite are the columns of St. John of Acre, with inscription in Latin dating as far back as the seventh century, accompanied by a red porphyry column, from which, in olden time, a herald proclaimed the law.

The bell tower, referred to, dates back to 903. It is 320 feet high, and contains the home of a watchman, who, at stated intervals, rings the bell. Among the paintings worthy of especial mention, is that of "Paradise," 84x33½ feet, by Tintoretto, said to be the largest canvas in the world, and one of "Venice in the Clouds," by Paul Veronese. The home of Shakespeare's Shylock is now a pawn-broker's shop, and Othello, or Christopher Moro, lived here on Campo del Carmine. Both Titian and Tintoretto had houses here, as did also Marco Polo, the renowned traveller. Monuments to Canova and Titian can be seen in St. Maria Gloriosa. The church St. Maria della Salute, before mentioned, has a history. In 1630, 60,000 inhabitants were carried away by a pestilence, and, on its disappear-

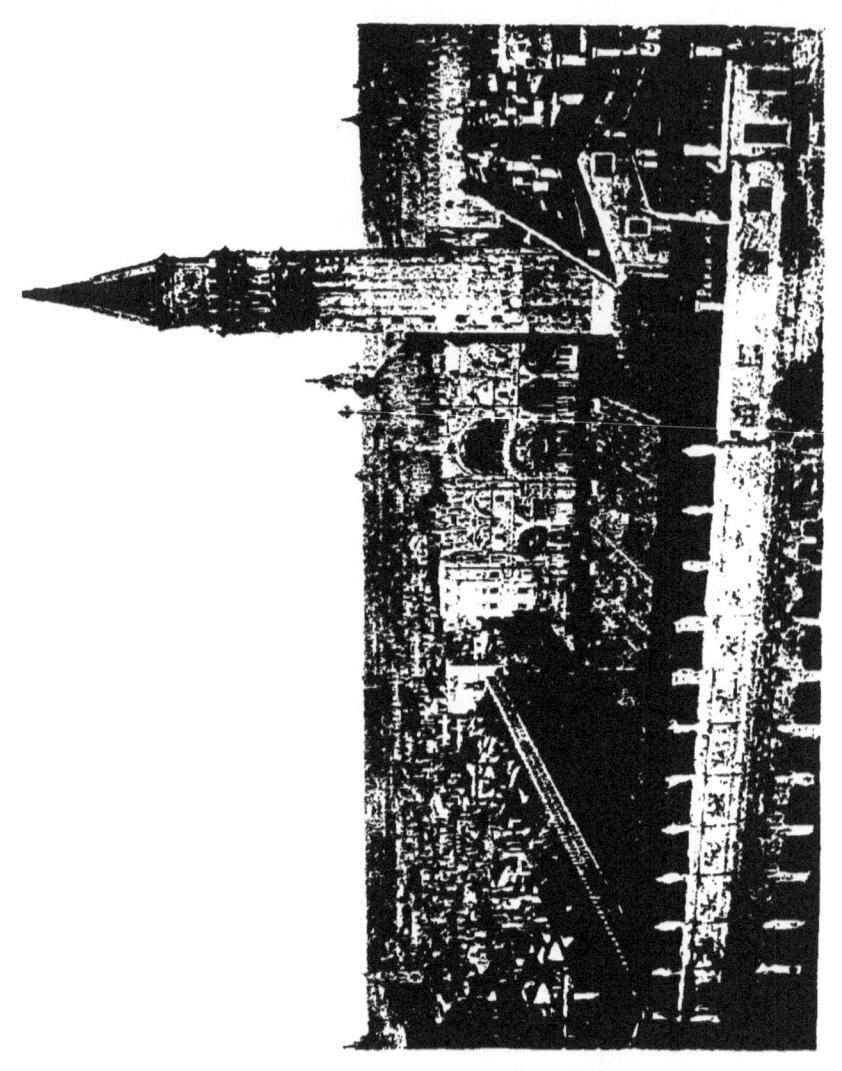

ST. MARK'S SQUARE, CATHEDRAL AND CAMPANILE.

ance, the Venitians erected this vast edifice in gratitude. It faces upon the Grand Canal, near its eastern mouth, and though somewhat dilapidated in its outer statuary, is considered the most magnificent church in the whole city. It contains Titian's "Descent of the Holy Spirit," and Tintoretto's "Marriage of Cana," also a flag and pacha's tails captured from the Turks. In the Academy, a little to the west, is Titian's finest production, the "Assumption." But with all the relics of the past, we find their modern lace and glassware in close and successful rivalry. In fact, it is fully as marvellous and interesting. To one acquainted with the four to six foot streets of Venice, and the absence of every sort of vehicle, the origin of head transportation, so common with the Italians in America, seems self-evident.

When visiting a foreign city for the first time, it is well to see the people as they live, and although difficult, as in Venice, you lose a good part of the real benefit of the trip unless you take a stroll around the streets and by-ways. You are hardly out of sight of one church before you fall in with another. As I looked up the Grand Canal, the magnificent tower of one stood, like some in Benares, inclined to the stream at an angle of 60 degrees, and probably has so stood for years. If you are not careful in the selection of your gondola, your personal comfort will be much greater on the narrow walks than on the water-ways, as they often take you by the shorter routes through scenes and odors most execrable. If it were not for the daily tide here, it would be impossible for man to breathe. No one can realize the vast accumulation of filth of all kinds which such a large city produces. Sixty thousand of its people were once lost by pestilence, but how far traceable to this cause is not known.

It was raining when I, in company with an English clergyman, took the train in departure, and was whirled out into mid-ocean, it seemed, towards solid land and Verona. It was soon reached, however. It is located on both banks of the Adige, and has many splendid edifices. Here Shakespeare has again immortalized an Italian locality in his "Romeo and Juliet." A public house is shown you as the residence of the Capulet family, the family of the loving but unfortunate Juliet, and in a neighhoring garden is a chapel said to contain her remains. But never mind, we do not believe everything we hear. Where is Romeo? Verona is known as the home of Pliny, who died while philosophically trying to solve the outbreak of Vesuvius in 79. Paul Veronese also was born here, as were the Scaligers. It is beautifully surrounded with fields of grain, fruit and flowers. Its silk factories are numerous, and exports of raw silk very large. Just below at Mantua, Virgil was born. While on my way we stopped at Padua, the oldest city in northern Italy, and possessor of one of the oldest universities in the world. Dante once lived here, studying at the University with Petrarch. Galileo held a professorship here, and Harvey in 1602 was here graduated. I did not make a stay as it seemed less interesting and cleanly than other points farther on. As I went on towards Milan, Solferino, well known for its battle of 1859. soon came in sight, a little south of Lake Guarda.

When I opened my eyes one lovely autumn morning and looked upon the clean streets and fresh marble and stone buildings of Milan, I thought I had never seen in the whole world so neat and beautiful a city. Time has not changed my mind. The air was fresh from the snow-crowned Alps, quite visible in the distance, and bright-green shrubbery filled park, avenue and garden. Its magnificent Cathedral, the bride of the earthly church, so strongly typical of religious truth and purity, sat in fairest white awaiting our heartfelt adoration. Is it inspired! It certainly inspires you. What hath man wrought! There it rises, of pure white marble, 490 feet long and 180 feet wide. The more you gaze, the more deeply you feel the impossibility of adequate description. In fact, it is a long while before you can grasp the hundreds of pinnacles, spires and statues, and at last you find the eye running in bewilderment over its clouds of delicate tracery as if it were a vision. Nor is the effect less entrancing when you enter. Its clusters of pillars supporting the vault 90 feet above, its countless marble figures, its bright walls and lofty arches, all blend into the realm of the wonderful. Here they will show you a nail from the cross, some thorns from the crown, and a piece of the purple robe of Christ, the rod of Moses, and some of Daniel's and Abraham's teeth. These things jar upon your highly-wrought nerves as trumpery, for you can feel no faith in them, and you hasten outside again, where nothing can disturb your meditations.

The rising sun tints the countless pinnacles and magnificent tracery with rosy light till the beautiful structure seems alive with delicate coloring. The works of nature are so perfect, were there no history of its erection, it would be easy to believe that it sprang from the earth. Such a wonder can grow, but is seldom made. Why Napoleon never removed it to Paris, exceeds my comprehension; everything else he could lay his hands on travelled that way. It must have been that he thought it would do just as well after he had conquered the world. Twice has Milan been taken by the French, once in 1796, and again after Marengo. The Simplon road commences here at the Arch of Peace, a fine marble structure 73 feet long and 74 feet high, with a bronze statue of Peace drawn in a car by six immense horses.

The Church of St. Maria della Crozier still contains on its walls the masterpiece of Leonardo Da Vinci, 30x15 feet, "The Last Supper." After the battle of Marengo, the soldiers used this room for a stable, and the labor of sixteen years of Da Vinci's life was for a time threatened with destruction, but it fortunately escaped, and now its disturber, Napoleon I, has a fine statue by Canova in close proximity. To speak of Milan's art collections, or places of interest, would require a whole volume. Suffice it to say also, that as a place of business, it is a model for other Italian cities and, I believe, for the rest of the world. A little west and south are the historic fields of Magenta and Marengo, the latter being one of the closest of Napoleon's battles, both in severity of the contest and in loss of able men.

A COIN FROM JERUSALEM.

CHAPTER IX.

Beneath the dome of heaven's pure blue, amidst eternal snow,
The glistening ice-fields at our feet, the smiling vales below,
    On Alpine peaks we stand.

It was late Autumn when I left Milan for Switzerland. Hardly had I got beyond its walls when my eye caught sight of the pretty lakes that make Italian scenery so celebrated. I was soon in Como, located at the southern end of a long, narrow lake, way down in the valley below, sparkling with blue and white so beautifully, I thought I had never seen anything so lovely, unless above the whirlpool below Niagara Falls. There the narrowness of the walls or banks of the river often give the same beautiful azure to the leaping water in the deep abyss below. Queen Caroline's old residence stands before you, once known as the Villa d' Este, and the picturesque loveliness of the surrounding heights is too grand for expression. And yet, nestled down in the valley is a city of about 25,000 people, with double walls, and actively engaged in manufacture of silk, cotton and woolen goods. You realize but one thing, and that is, the sublimity of its mountain scenery. It seems like the connecting link between the mighty Alps and the fertile plains. Vegetation runs to the very summit of these hills, and one of its prettiest sights is that of a clear white marble villa peeping out from its surrounding orange, citron and mulberry groves. When you reflect that the lake is 35 by 2½ miles, you form but a faint idea of its real effect. Even in midsummer you have but to mount one of its hills to see the snow-crowned peaks of the distant Alps.

> "Sublime, but neither bleak nor bare,
> Nor misty are the mountains there,
> Softly sublime, profusely fair ;
> Looks out the white-walled cottage here,
> The lowly chapel rises near."

On leaving Como the air became gradually cooler. Chiasso and then Mendrissia soon came in view. At the latter place the ice and snow-capped Alps seemed quite near. We soon crossed Lake Lugano, and came to the place of the same name on its northern border. None of these Italian lakes are wholly in view at the same moment, and in that lies a great deal of their attractiveness. They are as winding and narrow as they are intensely blue. From here to Bellinzona the green landscape and the heavily laden vine keeps your attention riveted. Strong, rosy women and girls trudge over the fields and along the single road to their distant home, with tall wicker baskets strapped to the back filled to the brim with luscious grapes. You want to stop and run through its green fields and shady groves as light-hearted as its people. Lake

Maggiore, with its long, narrow strip of bluest water, is away to our left, dotted here and there with little sail-boats as white as the villas hanging to the hillsides Bellinzona is the largest place just before reaching the St. Gothard Tunnel. Its importance arises in part to its being the junction of four railroads.

I was soon on my way to Switzerland over the towering snow-crowned Alps. Although I had the choice of two carriage roads, one over the Splügen Pass on the east, and that over the Simplon Pass to the west, I preferred to try the Mt. St. Gothard Pass and its celebrated railroad, and soon after leaving the last named station we gradually began our tortuous ascent to the clouds. St. Bernard Pass and Mt. Blanc loomed up away to the southwest. Slowly but surely up we went, and on looking down I wondered why the valleys below were so full of railways. It was not long before I found that away up above us were not only other lines but tunnels, and began to see that they were all but a part of the one circuitous route I was pursuing. Still up, up, up, we went, now climbing into a dark hole in the mountain, and then crawling out into daylight, till we found ourselves viewing again and again the same low valley or snow-capped peak, like so many new scenes.

For over nine miles, we were in the heart of the mountain in one continuous tunnel. The infant Rhine rolled down the steeps on my right, while to my left splashed and gurgled the rills that start the mighty Rhone. Hundreds of feet above, waterfalls burst over the rocks, fell into mist and soared away in clouds. The region of perpetual snow on my left shone like burnished silver. There was the noble Finsteraarh, 14,026 feet; Shreckhorn, 13,394 feet; and Jungfrau, 13,761 feet, flanked by others of as great, if not greater height. Away to the southwest were Monte Rosa, 15,217; Matterhorn, 14,705; and Weishorn, 14,804 feet. The modest hospice of St. Gothard, perched like an eagle in its loneliness, appeared on my left just before entering the tunnel, and the hospital and Devil's Bridge back to the left of our exit at Oberalp.

From the thrifty farms and fertile fields up the giant peaks, through chestnut groves laden with ripe fruit, past picturesque cowherd with patient drove quietly grazing on the hills, still up past flocks of goats nibbling to the very snow line, we labored on. The tinkling of bells and the plash of the waterfalls, alone, broke the quiet air. From the plank house with first story of stone for a barn, to the rough log building with its long overhanging roof, we came to the desert, the wilderness of the air. The trees grew less tall and drooped their thick branches as if perennial snow and rain had destroyed all their buoyancy. Long lines of firmly imbedded posts and interwoven branches and vines stood far up from the railroad to protect it from avalanche or rush of spring torrents. Now and then a group of picturesque dwellings nestled or clung to a little green plain where none but the mountain eagle or vulture can live in safety, and every boom that startles your hearing brings sad forebodings of disaster. Like a mist, the light snow rises and reveals a solid cloud of white where, but a few minutes before, all was lovely green. And thousands of feet below on the pretty level farms, men, women and children are making their autumn hay and gathering fruit. Fine plump cattle and sheep quietly graze in the rich pastures and beside the blue waters, as if the world held naught but health and peacefulness.

At 2 P. M. I was at Goeschenen, the first village beyond the tunnel, in Switzerland, in a light snowstorm, but passed right on to Altorf, the capital of the Canton of 'Uri, and memorable for the traditional shot of William Tell immortalized by Schiller. The patriot's reputed birthplace, Bürglen, lies a little to the east. Altorf contains the oldest Capuchin convent in Switzerland. It is romantically located near the Bay of Uri, and never wearies with its grand and lovely views. Not far beyond, we come to Flüelen, on the same sheet of water, and containing Tell's chapel, and still further on to Schwyz, the capital of the canton of the same name. Besides being interesting on account of being the scene of the early struggles of the Swiss against their Austrian oppressors, from Altorf down they are memorable for the retreat of the Russian Army before the French in 1799.

Wide on both sides extend the green fields, full of fine plump cattle and sheep. Even vegetables and wheat yield abundantly. As I alight, a buxom dame and daughter stand viewing my train, with the most pronounced admiration of the whole equipment. Their cheeks were like roses, and well worthy of returned admiration, which they undoubtedly received. Everything in Switzerland has the appearance of perfect health, and yet here the barns, for stabling all their domestic animals, are built beneath the same house that is to shelter the family. In pleasant weather, you seldom find a woman's head protected, and they would laugh at the idea of corsets. Man as I am, I envied them in their happy consciousness of health and strength. And that is not all, for health often means content and good nature. Well may they love their green fields, deep blue lakes and Alpine peaks! Stranger as I was, it made me homesick to depart. Goldau and the Rigi somewhat consoled me. Lake Zug, at your feet at the north, and Lake Lucerne on the south, with bright little Küssnacht nestling in the green, level valley, is a panorama never to be forgotten.

With Alpine stocks, like so many brave shepherdesses, some ten young ladies accompanied us to the small railway, and when seated in the car looked the perfect picture of healthy country life. Some were

English, some French, and a few German, but not one, however pale at home, failed to rival the others in the roses on their cheeks or the firmness with which they grasped the Alpine crook. The ascent is not very long, but slow, as the grade is 250 per 1000 feet, and rises from Lake Lucerne 5,739 feet. None regretted the ascent, even though snow was rapidly falling, and cold, unwelcome tremors ran through one's precious body in spite of stern determination to appear nice and comfortable. It was but a few weeks before that I was broiling under an Arabian sun, and longing for just such a climate. Yet I was happy in my misery, for others were colder than I, and threatened the frequent overturning of the car, when at times they found it impossible to longer remain desperately impassive, and suddenly, with a sudden "Oh dear!" went off into a convulsive shiver that shook us all into loud laughter.

On my descent, I went on to Lucerne, the chief place in the canton of that name. It lies at the head of Lake Lucerne, in the midst of cultivated hills and grand, distant mountains. It is partly surrounded by an ancient wall with octagonal towers, one of which once served as a light-house to the Lake, hence its name. From merely a monastery, it has gradually grown to a city of 18,000 souls. It still has two of its ancient covered wooden bridges spanning the river, and also a work of interesting art in its "Lion" by

Thorwaldsen, commemorating the members of the Swiss Guard who fell defending the Tuilleries in Paris in 1792.

The Lake of Lucerne extends for eight miles its narrow and beautifully irregular course, between steep mountains rising from 4000 to 5000 feet above, and, making a sharp bend south, becomes the Bay of Uri before referred to. As many as four large hotels testify to its growing importance as a summer resort. There are also small steamers regularly running up and down its pretty surface. Apart from the rare loveliness of hill and plain, lake and river, many deeds of memorable heroism tend to rivet the Swiss to his native land. This it is what keeps contentment in their homes and unity in their government. Their early struggles for liberty against Austria, so dearly bought, still remains a lesson to keep from war and bloodshed. The Roman army, Napoleon's army, the Russian, and the Italian have all scoured the country to and over the Alps, but, like spring following winter, the warm rays of peace have made her fertile valleys again blossom like the rose. The common dwelling is made of four corner posts, filled in between with plank or stone, while up the steep Alpine heights, none are seen but the rude formation of one log notched and laid upon another. The low, overhanging roof, however, redeems it from unsightliness, and even, with its surrounding drooping firs, presents a scene strongly picturesque. How can a people breathe in such a land and not be free!

From here I went to Sempach, where the leagued cantons defeated Austria. It is a small place quietly located by a little lake of the same name. I was next at Zurich, at the head of the pretty Lake Zurich. It is a large place for the country, numbering about 76,000 people. It has a university and a fine art school. She it was, years ago, that offended Germany by lavish praise of the English poets, Milton and Shakespeare. Although in a plain, it joined the mountain cantons for liberty. Crossing the Aar at Brugg, I was soon in Basle, quite on the frontier of Alsace. Here I found myself by the noble Rhine once more. Here, again, is a university, and an old Gothic cathedral bearing date of 1010, and containing the tomb of Erasmus and other eminent divines; for theology has always held sway here since the days of Cop and John Calvin, who studied and carried on their crusade against the weaknesses of the Catholic clergy here. Here was started, in 1804, the first Bible Society on the Continent. Silk, cotton and woollen goods are largely manufactured, but its chief trade is in ribbons. The battle of St. Jacob took place in its vicinity, and since the old Romans first located the outpost, its vicissitudes in times of war have been many. In 1431 a council to reform the Church was here held. In 1437 the council ordered the Pope to appear before them at this place, and he replied by proroguing the council. Still the council continued its sittings and reprimanded his Holiness for his disregard. It seems to have been a struggle between the universities or seats of learning and the papal chair, and after the appointment of a rival Pope, and death of the incumbent, harmony was brought about by a compromise. Much of interest might be added to these few words, but I am in haste to get away from the chilly air and view the blue Alsatian mountains beyond.

The next day I reached Mülhausen, the chief place in upper Alsace. The south of the town is prettily laid out in promenades, but some of the other portions are far from attractive. It is an old mediæval town, but little but its town-house shows the marks of age. Several wealthy families have, for years, monopolized the manufacture of muslins and calico printing. There is a system of workingmen's homes, similar to that in America, where the laborer may obtain a neat, complete home by paying a certain sum monthly from his wages. The people, at the close of the Franco-Prussian war, began to emigrate, on account of their strong French sympathies, but as time goes on she may regain her loss from other nations.

About seventy miles north, after passing through Colmar with its old cathedral of 1363, I came to Strasburg, the stronghold of the Rhine, surrounded by green fields, and lifting to the sky its vast cathedral towers to the height of 465 feet. Instead of suffering from its severe bombardment in the late war, it seems to have expanded and put on the appearance of new, wide streets and modern style of architecture. The old part has streets too narrow for comfort or convenience, and is a type of a mediæval town. Part of its cathedral dates back to 1015, but the spire was not finished till over 400 years after. Gutenburg spent a part of his life here, an event now commemorated by a statue. There is one also to Gen. Kleber, who was born in the place. The old university lies a little to the east of the cathedral, and is now in a flourishing condition. About 90,000 dwell within the new walls and fortifications of the city, and near the university is stationed the 15th corps of the German Army. Before the war of 1870-71, a large part of the people were Germans, but really sympathized with France, which led to a large emigration to Canada and the United States, as soon as their conquerors enclosed Alsace within the German lines. For a military town of the first magnitude its trade is curious, consisting of pates de foie gras, or "fat liver pies," to the amount of $500,000 annually, hops, sausages, hams and sauerkraut.

From three to five miles from the centre of the town, at certain intervals, the Germans have put a circle of fourteen forts, thus greatly strengthening it as a strategetic point. The old pentagonal citadel of 1682 was totally destroyed in the Franco-Prussian war. The 8th

Roman Legion was once stationed here, then called Argentoratum. In 1349, for alleged poisoning of the wells of the town, 2,000 Jews were burnt to death. The peace of Ryswick in 1697 gave Alsace and Strasburg to the French, but after a siege of seven weeks 17,000 of the French Army surrendered the place to the Germans in 1870. During a part of the engagement, ten to fifteen shells were sent into the town per minute. At night, soldiers could read ordinary print four miles distant by the light of the burning Public Library, the new Temple, Museum of Painting, and many other fine buildings. Everything has been cleared away, till now there is no appearance of the deplorable ruin. Twenty thousand people were left without homes or money. There were not 300 houses in the whole place uninjured.

From Strasburg, both Nancy and Marion were before me, but as I was quite familiar with the latter, I decided to pay a visit to the former instead. It is the old capital of Lorraine, and fell into the hands of the French at the same time with Strasburg. It now contains many of the Alsatians who left their native soil at the close of the late war, which so quickly returned nearly all but Nancy to the German fold again. They are now engaged in the manufacture of hosiery, fine embroideries and artificial flowers. It has, among other interesting institutions, a thriving University and many schools.

After passing by long white streets shaded with the tall Lombardy poplar, and over wide and level fields long since harvested, where many a brave soldier lost his life before Metz, I reached Chalons, an old provincial town that had twice, in the Middle Ages, repulsed the English from her walls, and once been capital in place of Paris. It has nineteen acres of fine park, which suffered severely in the Franco-Prussian war. The old woolen fabric called "Shalloon" originated here which, together with shoes, hosiery, cotton cloth, and its immense wine trade, constitutes the chief business of its active inhabitants. It has a Cathedral going back to the twelfth century, a Benedictine Abbey, and a host of other relics of the past. Attila was here defeated in 451. MacMahon was once located here, but it early fell into the hands of the Germans, and on account of its railroad facilities became an important aid to their final victory in 1872.

I had now come to a familiar part of France, so I took a midnight train for Creil, Amiens and Calais. The night was dark and rainy, the rain soon changing to hail and snow. An American lady, with two fine appearing young sons, was my only companion until we stopped for early lunch, when we found, on our returning, our compartment taken by two inveterate smokers, who had made it unfit for occupancy. Through Northern Italy and the whole of Switzerland, I had been fortunate in securing one of the two single upholstered chairs, now to be found on the left side of their compartment cars, which gave me all the accommodation of a drawing-room train. When daylight broke, the wide, fertile fields of Normandy, stocked with grain or covered with shivering cattle and sheep, lay spread out before me on all sides. Although it was away back in 1874 and 1877 when I had visited the country, everything seemed unchanged. Even Boulogne, with its old stone Cathedral on the hillside, and its high cross, where Napoleon with his large army pondered the feasibility of crossing to subdue England; and Calais, with its citadel, erected by Cardinal Richelieu in 1641, and its revolving light shedding its resplendent rays to the distance of twenty miles, appeared as quaint and dull as ever. Calais is well fortified, even having meadows on two sides capable of being quickly flooded in event of danger. A submarine cable is here laid under the Straits of Dover to England. The terminus of the proposed tunnel to England is six miles west. After the famous battle of Crecy, in 1346, Edward III. of England laid siege and gave it into the hands of England till 1550, when 30,000 men under the Duke of Gnise succeeded in retaking it.

Twice a day the English mail-boats steam across to Dover and return, and it is a pleasant pastime any warm, pleasant day to sit and watch this great thoroughfare of England, Norway, Sweden and Germany, as the different vessels constantly pass in review. The white-fringed caps of the fisherwomen peer out from under mounds of black fish-nets upon their bending shoulders, as they stride down to the sea. Women in frilled muslin descend from their two-wheeled bread and milk wagons and deliver their goods, even on Sunday, with little less grace than in their household duties. I again saw it all, as I had the Sunday in 1874, when first I trod the soil of France. But soon we were all aboard in search of a warm spot. No one, after looking at the high billows, cared to go below, so down on deck men, women and children soon ensconced themselves behind the solid rail. Once out in the Channel, a cross sea of immense billows steadily hammered our feeble starboard until it seemed impossible to go on, but by a slight inclination of the bows we succeeded in getting in sight of Dover Castle, and at last the high granite embankment of the town. The passage was but little more than an hour's duration, but, thank the Lord, it was no longer, or there would have been little left to some of us. Yet its yellowish-green billows, so fatal to happiness, are always beautiful here, and it was so icy cold it is a great wonder how seasickness could get a chance to work at all.

CHAPTER X.

The globe at last is won.
Adieu, good friends. Welcome grateful home!

F<small>ROM</small> Dover, I wished to take a turn to the west to see Hastings, where William the Conqueror in one short hour changed the destiny of England, if not the world; and the quaint old town of Lewes, connected, so many centuries ago with my name and ancestry. Lewes, the county town of Sussex, sits on a hillside, about seven miles north of the English Channel, on which it has a port called Newhaven. Its great antiquity is disclosed by the ruins of King Alfred's old castle on the height back of the town. One main street extends through the centre of the town, from which issue many little streets at right angles. The cliffs of chalk, so common in southern England, really form its location and surrounding country. Here it was that, in 1264, Simon de Montfort defeated Henry III. It was the royal stronghold and seat of the South Saxon kings, and Athelstan here established a mint that continued to the time of William the Conqueror. Until 1868 it returned two members to Parliament. In 1845, in the grounds of the old priory of St. Pancras dating 1078, were unearthed two ancient lead coffins, one containing the remains of William de Warren, who rebuilt the old castle here, and the other those of Gundrada. Roman coins are continually coming to light from the soil, and ancient mounds testify to its great antiquity. A remnant of the old Norman style of architecture is still seen in its Church of St. John. St. Anne's, also, is very early English. St. Michael's is bare and plain, but has some fine old monuments. For years the place has been celebrated for its iron and brass work, and some curious old specimens are still found in the latter church.

The names Lewes and Lewis are of the same derivation, both abridged and euphonised from the Latin appellation Ludovicus, through the Norman-French Louis. A few miles west is located England's most fashionable watering place, but as Brighton had no especial interest to me, my return to the London, Chatham and Dover R. R. was immediately made, and a train taken for the ancient town of Canterbury. Even then traces of snow lay on the sides of the track, but the sloping hills and green fields of Kent were still clear and beautiful. The little villages and isolated farm buildings, with the omnipresent round hop tower, in the absence of forest or grove, stood out in barest outline, and thousands of slender poles, still standing, like skeletons, in the wide gardens, disclosed that it is still a great hop-raising country. After leaving Dover, Canterbury is soon reached, and as you alight at the station, its undulating aspect at once attracts your attention. It is a city now, and the Archbishop of its ancient cathedral is primate of all England. Here the Romans built their town, Durovernum, and here Ethelbert held his court and made it the capital of all England. During his reign, in 596, Augustine arrived from Rome to introduce Christianity. In 1170 the unfortunate affair between Henry II. and Thomas a Becket, which ended in Becket's death in the cathedral, took place, and made Canterbury the Mecca of the whole country. This ran on until Henry VIII. destroyed the shrine of St. Thomas. Chaucer, writing in the fourteenth century, pleasantly represents the pilgrims leisurely sauntering along the highway, telling anecdote and story, and making it a holiday excursion. Even to this day we constantly use two words handed down therefrom : a canter, or easy pace, and a Canterbury tale, a fictitious narrative.

On one side of the station is the Martyrs' Field. On the other a tall round stone tower, surmounting a high mound, called Danejohn or Donjon, attributed to the early Celts. A little north are the old Norman Castle ruins, and further east, standing on the sight of a Roman temple given to St. Augustine and his followers by King Ethelbert, the famous old Cathedral. This church was destroyed, but rebuilt in 1070. Leaving out the proportions and history of the Cathedral, it awakens no deeper interest than St. Martin's, away to the southeast on St. Martin's Hill. This was the church of Bertha, Ethelbert's queen, before 596 and Augustine's arrival, and is probably the earliest church in all England.

Leaving Canterbury by the same road, the next point of interest was Rochester Castle, old and gray, almost square, perched upon a high elevation on the left. The river Medway peacefully flows between sloping banks of richest green at its feet. Its style is Norman, and it is said to have been built by Gundulph, Bishop of Rochester, in the eleventh century. Here King John, Simon de Montfort and Wat Tyler, each, in his day, laid long siege; and within its walls have been entertained Henry III., Henry VIII., Charles V., Queen Bess, Charles II. and James II. Yet there it stands, grandly surveying the beautiful landscape, bare, almost cruel in its lines, a patriarch of feudal ages still defiant of time. The smoke of London, St. Paul's dome, and the sluggish Thames come quickly into view after leaving Rochester, and then I felt at home. Years before, the land marks of the Tower, almost down by the water's side; St. Paul's; The Inns of Court by the old London Bar, now removed and replaced by a statue and tablets; Leicester Square, with its bust of my namesake, Sir Isaac Newton, prominent chin, straight, well-formed nose, and hair parted in the middle, and all, the innocent cause of many an unhappy hour in childhood, and still instant aggravator of my own insignificance; Charing Cross; Trafalgar Square; Houses of Parliament, Westminster Abbey, and Buckingham Palace had become familiar, so in a very few minutes I was at my hotel near the Square. In spite of my great fatigue, the quarter strokes of Big Ben in his high tower on the Houses of Parliament, and his solemn hourly peal, accompanied with the bar of music from St. Martin's, and distant call of still another, kept me wide awake till nearly daylight.

When I awoke it was as cold as Greenland, an icy chill penetrating to the marrow. It was quite early when, after breakfasting, I went out and found upon the rude seats and cold stone pavement around the fountains of the Square, scores of tattered men and boys sound asleep, their purple, sunken faces betraying the chill their ill-clad bodies were suffering. I had seen such an exhibition of great London's poor years since, and quickly recalled the noise and street disturbance of the night before. There had been a riot, a bread riot so called, and mounted police had been called out to ride down and dispel them. These were but a few specimens of the immense crowd of five hours before left asleep on the field. On the next Sunday, one of this very crowd walked boldly into Westminster Abbey, but a short distance from the Square, and interrupted divine service by publicly insulting the Dean. Shall I prolong my story? My object in writing at all is merely to jot down in a fragmentary way what may occur to me of my long and happy trip Conscious that I have omitted many interesting experiences, and that too little care has been taken in relating what I have really given, I have now arrived as near the end of my tale as I have to the end of my long journey.

After my usual service at St. Paul's, and a run through Western England, out upon the cool sea, far from the chilly, smoky land, I at last find time to rest and reflect.

Hardly hours away from shore, when, while promenading the hurricane deck and trying to get my sea-legs on, there came a sudden lunge of the steamer, and I saw something drop from above strike heavily on the rail, and disappear into the boisterous waves below. With an effort, I gained the side and saw the bloody and frightened face of a man just rising above the surface. The officer on deck was by my side in an instant, and the captain and officer on the bridge at the same time discovered the accident, but it was some little time before we were aware that anything was to be done for the poor fellow's rescue. He could yet be seen trying to wave his hand to catch our attention. A few men ran to the davits and began to leisurely cut the cords of a boat's covering. It looked as though an order had been given merely for repairs. No attempt was made to turn about, and only a slight change was noticed in the vessel's speed. The covering of the boat was not removed, however, and in a few minutes the vessel was racing on as before, and a poor, disabled mortal left alone in the cruel power of certain death. "Some vessel may pick him up," the officer said. That possibility did not, could not exist, to be of any avail, except to his dead body. Was it business! Was it because the will of one man, or even a majority, must rule! We all may be forced by circumstances to sacrifice, at the expense of justice or humanity, to this narrow and selfish doctrine so common in this world, and so deserving of punishment in the next, but no true man permits it long.

Several cold but pleasant days, in which the mighty billows lifted themselves bodily out of the water and sank in sheer exhaustion suddenly back again, now followed. Each morning the sun rose sparkling in the cold, clear horizon like an immense sapphire. I was fast nearing home. My watch and calendar, after varying nearly twelve hours fast, then slow, was gradually approaching true, standard time. My thoughts began to travel faster than my faculty of realization. In a few days—but stop! Two sailors are bearing towards the vessel's side a long, canvas-covered object strikingly like a heathen idol. It has a head, shoulders and shape like a human being. The burden is finally borne forward and rested on the bulwark. At sea any such object has a strong fascination, and captain, officers, doctor, steward, and a few weeping passengers soon approach and stand by its side. Then the old familiar scene of the sad part of ocean life forces my understanding. There is to be a burial! Some soul, less fortunate than ourselves, had, that morning, fled this clay, left it untenanted and forlorn.

The bell at my side begins slowly to toll out the years that breath and life have made their dwelling-place there. In solemn tones the Captain reads, "I Know that My Redeemer Liveth." Then a signal, a quick withdrawal of the National flag, a harsh, grating rasp, and heavily down into the pitiless, restless ocean depths plunged a helpless form. The closing billows leap and dance, and chase each other up and down over an unknown grave. Thus, within a few days' journey from home, an apparently healthy and strong young man had found a watery tomb, while I, after a long course of from 30,000 to 35,000 miles, in perfect health, still seemed destined to reach home in safety. An inscrutable Providence!

Soon the thick fog of the Newfoundland Banks closed densely in until, one morning, I was startled by the appearance of a bright light on our starboard bow. It was Cape Race Light, but 1,000 miles from New York. Two days later, we signaled our arrival off Fire Island, and before night saw Coney Island, Rockaway, and Sandy Hook nearly in front. We were in time to escape the bar, and by sunset stood off

Quarantine. A few minutes' delay, and we steamed by the Goddess of Liberty — whose benignant countenance I had bid good-bye so many months before, in grave doubt as to my ever seeing her bright face again, — my world-wide trip well ended.

INDEX.

	Page.
ACAJUTLA	38
ACAPULCO	42
ADEN	179
AFRICA	183
ALEXANDRIA	201
ANAM	113
ARABIA	179
ASPINWALL	23
BAHAMAS	15
BASLE	248
BENARES	158
BETHLEHEM	219
BORNEO	114
BURMAH	137
BRINDISI	220
CAIRO	207
CALAIS	253
CALCUTTA	147
CALIFORNIA	58
CANTERBURY	257
CANTON	103
CENTRAL AMERICA	29
CEYLON	108
CHALON	252
CHAMPERICO	41
CHINA	95
COLOMBO	169
COMO	240
CRETE	224
CUBA	17

ENGLAND	254
EGYPT	201
FLÜELEN	244
FRANCE	251
GANGES	154
GERMANY	249
GREECE	224
HAYTI	17
HEBRON	220
HONG-KONG	98
INDIA	143
ISMALIA	197
ITALY	226
JAMAICA	18
JAPAN	80
JAVA	118
JERICHO	220
JERUSALEM	217
JOPPA	216
JORDAN	221
KÜSSNACHT	245
LEWES	255
LIBERTAD	36
LONDON	258
LUCERNE	246
MADRAS	162
MALAY PENINSULA	117
MARION	251
MAZATLAN	51
MEXICO	42
MILAN	237
MT. SINAI	185
MÜLHAUSEN	249
NANCY	251

PADUA	236
PALESTINE	216
PANAMA AND CANAL	24
PENANG	128
PONDICHERRY	165
PORT SAID	200
PUNTA ARENAS	31
PYRAMIDS	210
RIGI	245
ROCHESTER	257
SAN FRANCISCO	59
SAN JOSE	38
SAN SALVADOR	36
SIAM	113
SINGAPORE	119
SOUTH AMERICA	20
ST. GOTHARD, ALPS, AND TUNNEL	142
STRASBURG	250
SUEZ AND CANAL	188
SUMATRA	118
SWITZERLAND	244
TOKIO	91
TURKEY	228
URI	244
VENICE	230
VERONA	236
WATLING'S ISLAND	16
YOKOHAMA	81
YOSEMITE VALLEY	66
ZANTE	224
ZURICH	247

www.ingramcontent.com/pod-product-compliance
Lightning Source LLC
Chambersburg PA
CBHW031250250426
43672CB00029BA/1915